The press about:

How the City Moved to Mr Sun - China's New Megacities
Michiel Hulshof & Daan Roggeveen

'Witty, poignant, startling...'
- *Duncan Hewitt, former BBC China correspondent*

'A delight to read.'
- *Architectural Record*

'Powerful accounts illustrating the unrivalled pace of change.'
- *De Volkskrant*

'Astonishing trip to urban jungle China.'
- *De Morgen*

Facing East: Chinese Cities in Africa
Michiel Hulshof & Daan Roggeveen

'The show's format is academic ... but the questions it raises about the alliance of two of the globe's fastest-growing geographic entities are not.'
- *The New York Times*

12 Good Ideas
for
The Future of Cities

The Amsterdam Agenda

Daan Roggeveen, Michiel Hulshof
& Frances Arnold

NAi010 Publishers

Index

Introduction 8
Michiel Hulshof, Daan Roggeveen

What Kind of City Do We Want To Be? 18
Esther Agricola

Bijlmer Blues 26
Daan Dekker

Participation Matters 38
Menno van der Veen

Digital Flexibility 46
Marc Schmit

Future of Work 58
Florian Idenburg

Flexible Systems 68
Selva Gürdoğan & Greger Thomsen

Smart Cities 78
Valerie von der Tann

The Grey Zone **90**
Neville Mars

Boring Hong Kong **102**
Inge Goudsmit

Irregular Development **116**
Adam S. Frampton

Planning for Migration **126**
Miguel Gentil Fernández

Over-tourism **138**
Stephen Hodes

Bright Lights, Big City **150**
David Mulder van der Vegt

Notes **158**

Biographies **162**

Acknowledgements **164**

Introduction

If you have been away from Amsterdam for a number of years, like us, there is one thing you will immediately notice upon your return: the city is doing well. *Very well.* At parties, home-owners furtively compare increased house prices. In no time at all, districts such as Bos en Lommer, the Indische Buurt, and Noord are turning into veritable paradises for lovers of coffee, yoga, and craft-brew beer. All of the major museums have been renovated. And after two decades of construction, the new subway connection running north-south through the city has finally opened. Professor of Urban and Regional Planning at the University of Amsterdam, Zef Hemel, goes so far to proclaim that the city is currently experiencing its "Third Golden Age" - after those in the seventeenth and nineteenth centuries.

Just three decades ago, the situation was rather different. Run-down buildings stood abandoned all over the city, crime rates were high, and heroin addicts openly shot up in the metros. Middle-class families preferred to live in safe, manicured dormitory suburbs like Purmerend or Almere. Quite simply, life in Amsterdam was anything but idyllic. By 1984, the population of the capital whole-heartedly sang along with young folk singer Danny de Munck's *Mijn Stad*: 'Amsterdam is dog poo on the pavements / And hatred in the streets / You've got to be on your guard / Especially late at night.'

Amsterdam's transformation has coincided with those of other major western cities, such as New York, London, and Paris. Rather than flee the chaotic, dirty, and oftentimes dangerous metropolis, people are now doing the reverse: ever-increasing numbers of knowledge workers, students, migrants, and tourists are moving into big cities.

But Amsterdam's change is nonetheless a double-edged sword. House prices are now so high that teachers, police officers, and nurses find it hard to secure accommodation in the capital. People might sit on waiting lists for social housing apartments for well over ten years. And there are other problems, too: plans to make Amsterdam more energy efficient are not delivering as they should. At the same time, a heated identity debate rages throughout the city, with an increasing number of citizens complaining about the influx of tourists, expats, and new yuppies. Meanwhile Amsterdam residents with migrant backgrounds are increasingly vocal about the fact that their culture must also be considered part of Amsterdam's urban identity.

These frictions are not unique to Amsterdam. Cities across the world face similar problems, making it a useful exercise to look for solutions from around the globe, be it Istanbul, Shanghai, or Berlin. This was the starting point of the Amsterdam Agenda, a series of lectures to second- and third-year students of the Amsterdam Academy of Architecture that took place in the spring of 2018. Across 15 lectures, international experts with specific insights into particular urban issues shared with students their research and analysis, presenting proposals and solutions from abroad that Amsterdam and the Randstad could learn from.

In this way, students were not only taken on a journey to a number of leading metropolises, but at the same time gained an understanding of the major urban challenges of our time: accessibility, sustainability, inclusiveness, and disruptive technologies. Our goal: to open up the discussion on the future of urban life and add new voices to the often self-referential debates in the Netherlands on this topic. We deliberately picked experts from different fields: architects and planners were joined by an activist, for example, a journalist, philosopher, and strategy consultant. Why? Because we think complex problems need to be looked at from multiples different angles.

We wanted to share the valuable insights of these 15 experts with a wider audience, so invited our editor, Frances Arnold, to examine their lectures, describe their narratives, and open them up to an even wider audience. The result is in your hands.

Context

Esther Agricola, Director of Urban Planning and Sustainability for the City of Amsterdam, outlined the huge task her department faces: building more dwellings without expanding the city. 'In Amsterdam, this hasn't actually been done before. In the past, each time the city boomed, we planned extension areas.' At the same time, society is rapidly changing through successive new technological possibilities. This makes urban planning, traditionally a very slow sector, much more difficult. Streets and buildings that are being planned today will still have to perform in 50 years. At a time when nobody knows what society will look like even a decade from now, this is a colossal challenge.

Currently, Amsterdam has roughly two extension 'flavours' to choose from. The first is large-scale housing developments that are planned top-down and in high density. The second takes a more fragmented approach, allows citizen participation in the planning process, and embraces the experiment *with* the city in its search for new and radical ideas. Model one is currently being applied in the Sluisbuurt, an area under development in the eastern docklands. Looking ahead, model two could be used in Haven-Stad, the largest ever urban expansion of Amsterdam, where the city is planning a partly car-free district with between 40,000 and 70,000 dwellings.

By letting international experts share their views on this challenge, we have arrived at an Amsterdam Agenda for the development of the city of the future. To summarize:

1. Take a step-by-step approach

Amsterdam's last visionary and radical urban development was the Bijlmermeer. Often described as Europe's final and fated experiment in Modernism, within a mere quarter-of-a-century its head designer, Siegfried Nassuth, witnessed not only its construction, but also the large-scale demolition of his life's work. Journalist Daan Dekker, author of *De Betonnen Droom (The Concrete Dream)*, illustrates how the Bijlmermeer's legacy holds valuable lessons for the Amsterdam of today. The problem wasn't the design itself, he explains, but the process. Under pressure from the high demand for housing, the radical design was rolled out almost in one go, without the possibility for adapting it to practical experiences.

2. Be radically transparent

Amsterdam's intention to grow by hundreds of thousands

of people inside the existing city limits means there are multiple interests, opinions, and vantage points to be taken into account. Legal scholar and philosopher, Menno van der Veen, specializes in various forms of citizen participation in spatial processes. He believes good and transparent processes help plan development, whereas a lack of participation opportunities can lead to protests and a standstill of progression.

3. Embrace permanent change

Architect Marc Schmit of the Berlin-based firm, playze, focusses on the transformative impact of digitalization on the city. Skype, Uber, Tripadvisor and Google Maps have transformed the way we navigate and understand cities. This enables a constant flux that calls for a type of planning that allows for a fluid form of multipurpose programming, and that can be reprogrammed time and time again.

4. Design atmospheres

Architect Florian Idenburg of the New York office, SO-IL, looks at the changing role of work in urban societies. Developments in technology, including robotics and AI, will render work less of an economic necessity and increasingly a lifestyle, he suggests. This poses several consequences for architecture. 'As an architect you have to focus more and more on the design of atmospheres: good spaces that are not linked to a specific use.'

5. Use informal systems

As well as proposing means of reinserting informal features back into planned environments, Selva Gürdoğan and Gregers Tang Thomsen of Istanbul office, Superpool, investigate informal forms of public transport in their city. Flexible, responsive, and comparatively low cost, in a city like Amsterdam where the construction of a new metro connection may take decades, this could present an interesting alternative model for future forms of public transport.

6. Be smart

Valerie von der Tann specializes in the role of technology in the development of smart cities. She examines how cities and their governments use technology and data to reach better decisions concerning the planning of the future - and how these can actually improve the lives of residents. Building on existing physical infrastructure as part of a holistic approach to urban planning, she asserts that, 'If we get this right, I think smart cities will not be a dystopia, but deeply human spaces with a quality of life enhanced by technology.'

7. Densify

In order for cities to become more sustainable, densification is a must, argues Neville Mars of MARS Architects, based in Shanghai. He urges the authorities of Asian cities to densify within existing boundaries, rather than extend building frontiers to create endless "Grey Zones." Nebulous and hard to define, these poorly planned and poorly regulated areas are the result of insidious urban expansion. To halt their spread, he proposes a two-pronged approach focussing both on existing city centres, as well as the countryside beyond. With the Chinese urban model now being exported abroad, resolution of this pressing issue has never been more urgent.

8. Maintain diversity

Few cities present a better example of extreme densification than Hong Kong, where OMA architect, Inge Goudsmit, has carried out extensive research. She warns that a high population density will not automatically lead to lively neighbourhoods. In contrast to Hong Kong's public-facing image, she reveals large swathes of the territory to have an unexpectedly monotonous side. The large-scale development of gated communities, for example, creates an urban structure that is socially and economically fragmented. This 'concrete jungle segregation' leads to 'black holes' in the urban fabric. Something to avoid!

9. Map, explore, use

In *Cities without Ground: A Hong Kong Guidebook*, architect Adam Frampton of Only If mapped traffic flows of different levels throughout the Asian metropolis, including above- and below-ground walkways, both informal and formal. The project revealed that ad-hoc infrastructure is every bit as important for the functioning of a city as planned. The work led to a similarly alternative mapping of New York, uncovering overlooked and irregular-shaped plots that hold exciting potential for new housing prototypes. Using this alternative strategy could reveal overlooked possibilities for urban development.

10. Design for migration

In addition to issues related to housing and new technologies, social changes are also a challenge for the twenty-first century metropolis. The most pressing is perhaps the anticipated increase in migration flows - a development that regularly leads to tension and conflict. Architect Miguel Gentil Fernández of Baum Arquitectura in Seville carries out research into migration between North Africa and Spain. He argues there is a critical role for architects and planners in inventing ways in which cities should respond to this complex social situation.

11. Prepare for tourism

Beyond permanent migration, there is yet another international flow of people on the rise. Just like Barcelona, New York, and Berlin, Amsterdam's tourism industry shows no sign of slowing - but at what cost, asks tourism expert Stephen Hodes of LAgroup. A trained urban planner, he makes a plea for radical measures to get a grip on the growing phenomenon of over-tourism, concluding that if Amsterdam gets this right, it could become a model city in more ways than one.

12. Plan for nightlife

And what is a good city without lively nightlife? Architect David Mulder van der Vegt of Amsterdam office, XML, wrapped up the series with a lecture about the influence of the club scene on the DNA of cities. Citing the symbiotic relationship between the Radical Architecture of 1960s and 1970s Italy and cities' creative cachet, as well as examples from New York and London, he argues that vibrant nightlife is fundamental to an inclusive as well as creative city.

The Amsterdam Agenda brings together a variety of inspiring visions and sharp opinions held by a new group of international specialists. It hopes to generate a lively debate across disciplines and backgrounds, and challenges planners of tomorrow to expand their understanding of their profession.

Rich in their diversity, a common denominator of these experts is that they apply a research-driven approach with studies either inside or outside the academic world. They also share a global perspective of the issues on which they work, and combine insights and approaches from different parts of the world. They demonstrate a hands-on, do-it-yourself approach, and all of them undertake self-initiated projects in a collaborative way. We feel this is indeed a new international generation of urban thinkers.

It is a key takeaway that, despite the distance or differences in governance, many of the world's most dynamic cities face similar challenges - be it the explosion of real estate prices, keeping pace with super-fast technological changes, sustainability, or identity. At the same time, it's clear that one size does not fit all. Rather, viable solutions to today's most pressing urban challenges depend greatly on local conditions. Nonetheless, examples from other cities always offer inspiration, as they broaden our range of prospects for action.

Amsterdam is on the verge of one of the biggest construction challenges of its history. The city has a long and proud tradition of embracing and absorbing people and ideas from all over the world; this is rooted deep in the capital's DNA. In laying out the hurdles, issues, and possibilities felt by other major world cities, it becomes clear that its planners of both today and tomorrow must continue to benefit from ideas, plans, and experiments from the rest of the urbanizing world.

Daan Roggeveen
Michiel Hulshof

'It's embedded deep in the DNA of the city,' says Esther Agricola, Director of Urban Planning, City of Amsterdam, of the Dutch capital's historical approach to designing its spatiality. 'There's the possibility to accommodate dynamics, new influences, and cultures. That capacity has been there for more than six hundred years. This city can absorb change. As urban planners we see it as our task to preserve that quality.'

Esther Agricola/ City of Amsterdam

What Kind of City Do We Want To Be?

Amsterdam is not a very large city. Its metropolitan area houses no more than 2.4 million people, its urban core less than one million. The city has a village-like charm, and is small enough to walk or cycle almost anywhere. But at the same time it is also one of the world's global cities, a primary node in global economic, cultural, technological, social, and other networks. Case in point: according to the 2018 edition of The Global Power Index, an annual ranking of major metropolises based on their, 'power to attract people, capital, and enterprises from around the world,' Amsterdam placed sixth after London, New York, Tokyo, Paris, and Singapore.[1]

But if Amsterdam is to retain its position, it must remain capable of absorbing change. Throughout its almost 750 year history, Amsterdam has excelled in this regard. However, just like other world cities, the financial crisis of 2008 put the Dutch capital on edge. The authorities reacted with an almost complete development stop. 'It was deemed too risky,' Agricola recalls. 'For the first time in 30 or 40 years we were confronted with empty areas without developments.' And yet, unlike elsewhere, Amsterdam rode out the crisis largely unscathed: the number of inhabitants kept growing at a rate of 10,000 to 12,000 people per year, and the economy grew at a steady rate.

'On the one hand we stopped building. On the other,

we were facing growing numbers of households and companies,' explains Agricola. 'This created a lot of tension in space, real estate and housing prices.' It meant that when the city administration asked the Department of Urban Planning to create a new strategy for Amsterdam four years ago, Agricola and her colleagues had much ground to cover. The main question to be addressed: *How to accommodate growth?*

To return to The Global Power Index's top six cities, it is useful to consider what sets these urban centres apart from the rest. Arguably, it is that they excel in accommodating alteration. It is like applying Charles Darwin's evolution theory of "survival of the fittest" to urbanism: as with living species, the *fittest* cities are not necessarily the strongest, biggest or even most intelligent. Instead, they are the most adaptable.

Amsterdam has managed to absorb enormous changes: the industrial, democratic, and technological revolutions that have made today's world very different and much more interconnected than that of 400 years ago. Yet the structure of the city was developed centuries ago; its citizens still live, work, and play in streets, squares, and buildings that are in many cases hundreds of years old. Hence, as a city in transition, Amsterdam represents an important case study, and potential template for others.

Although each unique in terms of culture, context, and just about everything else, today's leading cities all share common challenges. In order to meet the demands of the twenty-first century, not only must cities share solutions with each other, the planning discipline must also shift: 'More than ever we should introduce new expertise into our field,' urges Agricola.

'The biggest question Amsterdam needs to address is: what kind of city do we want to be? We are often discussing the need for new dwellings, economic development, or infrastructure, but that's not the debate we should have,' explains Agricola. 'We should talk about the character of the city, what do we want to keep and what should change? The answers to those questions have consequences for urban typology, for architecture. Not the other way around.'

Amsterdam: A History of Expansion

During the course of history, Amsterdam has doubled in size multiple times during periods of economic prosperity. During the seventeenth century, Amsterdam's first "Golden Age" was prefaced by the end of the Eighty Years' War: it saw Dutch art, science, and in particular, trade, prosper. Like a magnet, the powerhouse city of what was then the Dutch Republic attracted an influx of workers and thinkers, resulting in Amsterdam almost tripling in size. Later, in the nineteenth century, the Industrial Revolution saw Amsterdam's numbers swell yet again. Its continued contemporary growth, and that projected in line with the global trend for urbanization, has been dubbed a "Third Golden Age." What lessons, then, can the city learn from its past expansions, asks Agricola.

According to Agricola, Amsterdam's urban morphology can be read, 'like the rings of a tree. They're consistent, and the lines are still there,' she says. In the seventeenth century, for example, Amsterdam used the model of concentric canals in the old city. Later, in the interbellum between the First and Second World Wars, architect Berlage developed his distinctive urban plan of wide boulevards and high-density housing to meet the demands of a mix of classes in the city centre. And in the postwar period, Amsterdam broke with tradition again: 'The garden cities represented another very different urban pattern, with open planning and open urbanism,' explains Agricola.

'As urban planners we have to work with these existing systems,' she continues. 'We have to build alongside them.' In Amsterdam, these different urban systems are strictly separated: there is its canal district at its heart, wrapped by those elegant boulevards and garden cities, with towering high-rises along its edges. The clear distinction is a result of the city's strong public planning system - its urban planning department has been in existence for over a century - but there are also several other factors working in Amsterdam's favour. In particular, its *Erfpacht*, or ground lease system in which most the land is owned by the government, makes it relatively easy for urban planners to coordinate and stimulate building activities, as well as social amenities.

In recent years, Amsterdam has been developing in a new direction: upwards. 'We see more and more high rises. The city will have a totally new skyline ten years from now,' states Agricola.

A New Spatial Strategy

In its most recent urban vision, Amsterdam formulated several clear principles to accommodate sustainable urban growth. They included enlarging the inner city to release pressures of overcrowding; developing the city around the

IJ River and the harbour; enlarging the financial district along the South Axis; and finally, keeping Amsterdam green. But although the strategy still works adequately today, the government-imposed standstill on development during the financial crisis, combined with unwavering growth, means a new plan is now urgently required.

In 2014, the Department of Urban Planning developed a new vision for the future. An exciting opportunity, its actors nonetheless set one clear parameter from the outset: 'We cannot extend the city in area size. We will not invest in suburbia, but instead in densification within the existing urban fabric,' asserts Agricola. Initial research revealed that working within the city's existing limits would be eminently possible - 'But it would mean we have to work on transformations,' concedes Agricola. However, a clear advantage of urban transformation is that infrastructure, trains, parks, roads, and the like are already in place. A second advantage is sustainability. 'Densification is the best you can do for a sustainable city. That made it even more attractive to choose this strategy.'

One of the most visible spaces designated for urban transformation and densification is Haven-Stad, a large area that is currently in use as an industrial zone and harbour. One of the principle planned uses for the district is housing - something that Amsterdam urgently needs.

'Focusing on Haven-Stad, our current scheme allows for 40,000 to 70,000 extra dwellings. But we calculated that if you push it to the maximum, we can even build an additional 250,000 new housing units within the city limits. That means up to 600,000 more people. That's crazy if you realise that Amsterdam has 855,975 inhabitants today.

With our research, we showed growth is possible.'

So far, no problems. A city like Amsterdam, with a solid urban planning system and some 500 people working in the Urban Planning Department can surely just start building these extra dwellings, roads, and metro lines, right? Wrong: 'We discovered that in areas other than housing, we have reached a limit. It is not that easy at all,' says Agricola. 'To put it more dramatically: we have a huge problem at this moment.'

A very visible problem is that of mobility. Built in the nineteenth century, Amsterdam's transportation system is simply not up to the challenge of signifiant population growth. Illustrating her point, Agricola recalls a recent and relatively minor fire in the city's Schipholtunnel, close to the airport. 'This little fire closed the spare tunnel - not even the vital one - for a period of five hours. As a consequence, the traffic at Dam Square in the heart of Amsterdam had huge problems for 18 hours. That shows how vulnerable our transportation system is.' In a city where it can take up to 15 years to build a new highway, and in the region of 30 for a new metro line, this is a significant hurdle.

A second challenge is the energy transition. Amsterdam wants to be free of fossil gas by 2050. 'That is a massive operation that costs a lot of space. We have to change a lot in the houses, offices, and under the streets. We have 30 years to realize this.'

Another problem the city faces is that of its increased popularity. More and more companies settle in Amsterdam, and most of them would like to be in the inner city due to the vicinity of shops, restaurants, parks, public transport, and beautiful historic buildings. This means pressure on the inner city is growing. Agricola: 'There is a lot of space around Amsterdam, but all companies want to be in the same spot because they see it as economic asset.' For the Urban Planning Department, then, a key challenge is introducing these attractive qualities into new urban districts, away from city centre.

It is not only businesses that are attracted to metropolises like Amsterdam; tourists are, too. A city with fewer than one million inhabitants, Amsterdam attracts more than 17 million tourists a year, and the number is growing fast. According to Agricola this is 'a natural phenomena' that seems unstoppable.

But the biggest challenge might be that the speed of planning cannot keep up with the speed of change. Amsterdam needs more houses, better public transport, and a more sustainable energy system *now*. 'It takes at least two years for a plan to see the light,' says Agricola, 'But the city is growing faster and faster and cannot wait for two years.'

'Dealing with all these phenomenons I see a paradigm shift. We need different systems. We have to work more holistically than ever. How to combine energy, mobility, sustainability and economics all in a new planning system? That is the challenge of my office.'

The last big urban vision – Modernism – failed in cities around the world. Why? Daan Dekker looked at the Bijlmermeer in Amsterdam to find an answer. His conclusion: the experiment was too big, too radical, and leaving no room for gradual improvements or steady adjustments. A new urban vision for the city should stimulate and combine experimentation, evaluation and implementation.

Daan Dekker/ Pakhuis de Zwijger

Bijlmer Blues

In 2018, residential neighbourhood the Bijlmermeer in Amsterdam marked its 50th anniversary with a programme of exhibitions, performances and events.[1] In recent years, the once notorious district has emerged as a dynamic, creative and highly international community. While there is much to celebrate, the Bijlmermeer's (or Bijlmer, as it is colloquially known) painful journey to its current condition cannot be forgotten. And nor should it, argues journalist and author, Daan Dekker.

The failings of what is now considered Modernism's final, ill-fated large-scale urban experiment reveals hard-learned lessons to a new generation of planners currently engaged in new urban visions for not just the Netherlands, but the world. By dissecting the well-intentioned ideals, motives and dreams of the Bijlmer's architect, Siegfried Nassuth, as well as the broader institutional shortcomings that saw his vision descend into infamy, Dekker outlines why the ambitious project was doomed to fail. In doing so, he illustrates what today's planners can do differently, and why integration, communication and adaptability are essential for building a true 'city of the future.'

With hindsight, a fundamental flaw of the Bijlmer was its sheer size. Originally planned to accommodate 100,000 residents, the project was ambitious from the outset - and with good reason. By the second half of the twentieth century, Amsterdam was facing an urgent housing crisis. The Second World War had put the brakes on the city's General Extension Plan of 1935, with construction of four new suburbs to the west of Amsterdam beginning only in 1951: Slotermeer, Geuzenveld, Slotervaart and Osdorp. Devised by Cornelis Van Eesteren, a key member of the Modern Movement and chairman of CIAM (Congrès Internationaux d'Architecture Moderne) from 1930 to 1947, the new neighbourhoods adhered to the model of "garden city," and were characterized by a mixture of high-, medium-, and low-rise buildings, with plentiful green space. On the completion of Buitenveldert to the south in 1959, Van Eesteren's original plan was complete.

However, still more dwellings were needed. The end of the Second World War had sparked changes in the Netherlands and Amsterdam: peace brought with it a renewed optimism with more couples marrying, and having babies. These new families didn't want live with older generations; they wanted to embrace freedom in every sense. Further driving the need for additional housing was an influx of Dutch citizens from a newly independent Indonesia, with the Netherlands formally recognizing the former colony's sovereignty in 1949.

It was against this backdrop of change that a graduate of Delft University of Technology, one Siegfried Nassuth, was given the job of a lifetime. With only four years' work experience to his name, the young architect and planner was named project leader of a team set up to create a new urban vision for Amsterdam. Its goal: to match not just the city's growing numbers, but also the hopes and possibilities of an evolving, post-war society. Nassuth had idealistic ideas for a radical new way of living, inspired by both a childhood in the then Dutch East Indies and a later idolizing of Modernism's key protagonists. Nevertheless, the Bijlmer didn't just fail, it would fast become a very public mirror to the Netherlands' societal shortcomings of the final three decades of the twentieth century.

Siegfried Nassuth

Born in 1922, Siegfried Nassuth enjoyed an idyllic childhood in the Dutch East Indies, now Indonesia. His father's work in the colonial police force saw the family move between rural locations throughout Java, with the remote postings affording the young Siegfried ample opportunities to explore the countryside around him. A keen Scout, he would regularly journey deep into the forests and jungle for days on end, foraging for food, building camps, and living wild.

In 1942, at 19 years old, the teen's freedom came to an abrupt end when Japanese forces invaded the Dutch East Indies. As prisoners of war, Siegfried and his father were sent to work on the Burma Railway. Known for its horrific working conditions, pervasive maltreatment of workers, sickness and starvation, an estimated 330,000 people died during the railroad's construction. Among them was Siegfried's father, who succumbed to dysentery after just a few months.

In August 1945, Imperial Japan surrendered. Two days later, the men who would become Indonesia's first President and Vice President respectively, Sukarno and Mohammad Hatta, declared independence. After enduring three long years of hardship, Siegfried was finally free. However, his home - the Dutch East Indies that was - no longer existed. Displaced, Siegfried had no other choice but to move to the Netherlands, where he joined his mother and brother in Delft.

Nassuth's enrolment to the University of Delft's Faculty of Architecture was driven by pragmatism rather than idealism. The alma mater of his brother, the young man reasoned that his sibling's study may lead to professional opportunities on graduating. But although Nassuth's first two years at the school were less than promising, the optimism and freedom of a post-occupation Netherlands was unfurling across the country - including academia. At the faculty of architecture, the air of change signalled a shift in power - from founder of the Traditionalist movement, Marinus Jan Granpré Molière, to new professor Cornelis Van Eesteren, a proponent of Modernism and the driving force behind Amsterdam's 1935 General Extension Plan.

In stark contrast to Granpré Molière's abhorrence of 'modern' materials - such as concrete, glass and steel - and upholding of national styles and traditions, Van Eesteren was an advocate for functionalism, and architecture's potential to create a better world and more harmonious society. Nassuth was inspired by his new professor and in the role of student assistant, continued to learn from his mentor and father figure.

In 1958, the professor helped his protégé secure a position with Amsterdam's Department of City Planning. Having been delayed due to World War Two, Van Eesteren's General Expansion Plan, developed in 1935, was only just being realized at this time, and its housing shortfall fully understood. The city council therefore looked to an area southeast of Amsterdam as a potential site for a new residential neighbourhood, settling on a rural, agriculture-heavy region some 15 kilometres from the city centre. Determined to build a new suburb to finally end the capital's longterm housing crisis, the ambitious proposal won the enthusiastic support of Joop den Uyl, then an alderman in Amsterdam and later Prime Minister from 1973 to 1977. And so, in 1962 the city council appointed none other than Siegfried Nassuth to lead a team of young, visionary architects to create the Bijlmemeer, a totally new and radically different neighbourhood for 100,000 people.

Welcome to the Bijlmer

Nassuth's masterplan for the Bijlmemeer saw dozens of identical medium-rise blocks, arranged across a vast site in a distinctive honeycomb configuration. This particular layout was significant: not only did it avoid buildings overlooking each other - residents would enjoy views of green areas, rather than into their neighbours' apartments - it also allowed each and every 120sqm home direct sunlight. This uniformity mattered to Nassuth: he believed all deserved the same circumstances and conditions from which to forge their own lifestyles.

Inspired by Van Eesteren's own ideas around the functional city - that is, the clear segregation and separation of functions and activities within an urban centre - as well as a desire to create freedom and space for people, Nassuth's plans for the Bijlmer featured elevated roads. Huge parking garages further freed up the neighbourhood's expansive ground level for pedestrians, with tubular walkways linking the concrete block parking facilities to apartment buildings.

In Nassuth's plans, both the Bijlmer's hexagonal layout, as well as its futuristic elevated roads, would combine to create the suburb's most distinguishing feature: vast areas of green open space, inspired, perhaps, by the planner's exotic childhood spent roaming the wilds of Java. 'Nature was dominant,' Dekker explains. 'Nassuth wanted people to wander outside, and feel like they were in a forest.'

The scale and ambition of the Bijlmer captured the zeitgeist of an increasingly progressive, confident Amsterdam looking to forge new ways forward and break away from the old. Contingents of city planners would travel from abroad to visit the behemoth site, eager to learn from the Netherlands' bold new vision. The wave of optimism associated with the proposed Bijlmer was further propelled by an excitable media (*De Volkskrant* hailed the development as, 'A unique point in the history of city planning.'); as well as glossy marketing materials to promote the new flats.

There was a genuine buzz surrounding the Bijlmer. Indeed, the promise of affordable homes, set in a green idyll, and created specifically for society's most forward-looking seemed almost too good to be true...

A Disappointing Reality

To say the realities of the Bijlmer did not match expectations would be a vast understatement. 'It wasn't a green paradise, it was a muddy island,' describes Dekker. Residential blocks were built in succession, and on completion, made immediately available to prospective buyers. Because of this, tenants started moving in to the Bijlmer as early as 1968 - long before Nassuth's neighbourhood was complete. There were no sidewalks, for example. Shops and stores only started appearing in the mid-1970s, and a long-promised metro connecting Bijlmer to central Amsterdam was delayed until 1977. But as quickly became clear, in order to function as Nassuth and his team intended, their suburb needed to be finished; there simply was no contingency plan for gradual growth and evolution.

Not all of the Bijlmer's initial shortcomings were entirely Nassuth's fault. Realizing the planner's vision called for seamless cooperation between Amsterdam's city council and selected construction companies. However, the patchy collaboration between these parties saw them seize significant control over certain elements of the project's outcome, process, and even design. On reviewing Nassuth's plans, for example, the municipal government voted to increase tower blocks' five-storey height in order to make apartments more affordable to buyers.

This cost-saving also extended to how towers were fitted-out, with the proposed number of elevators deemed too expensive and duly cut. A small change on paper, in reality its ramifications were glaring: fewer elevators meant more residents using each, thereby making breakdowns due to overuse more frequent. At a security level, hundreds of people per elevator made knowing each face impossible, adding to a growing sense of social unease at the Bijlmer. The most significant upshot of this modification was the extension of galleries connecting individual apartments, which greatly reduced the privacy of residents Nassuth intended. Simply put, the plan left no room for compromise.

From Forgotten to Infamous

As dissatisfaction spread among the suburb's pioneer tenants, so too did the Bijlmer's less than utopian reputation, dissuading the city's target middle class demographic from moving into the neighbourhood. Low occupancy forced a drop in apartment prices, attracting primarily those groups for whom a home in central Amsterdam was all but impossible. They included students, hippies, and a significant gay population, who unable to meet the family requirements of city centre housing, faced little choice and ongoing discrimination.

The issue of social mix and ghettoization came to the fore with the independence of the former Dutch colony of Surinam in 1975. An influx of Surinamese people soon arrived in the Netherlands, all demanding housing. Many were placed in the Bijlmer, its concentration of concrete blocks presenting very different living conditions from their former Caribbean home. In a significantly less diverse Amsterdam than that of today, the Bijlmer became known as a predominantly black district.

Cut off from the rest of the city, by the early 1980s, the Bijlmer had become a repository for Amsterdam's most pressing social issues. The arrival of heroin to Amsterdam, for example, saw drug-related crime rise exponentially. Its shadowy garages, poor surveillance and visibility, as well as high levels of unemployment, made the Bijlmer its de-facto epicentre.

By the early 1990s, plans were being mooted to demolish a series of the Bijlmer's residential towers, which at the time numbered just 31 - a fraction of the number originally planned by Nassuth. However, tragic events of 1992 catapulted the area's intrinsic social dysfunction to global recognition, forcing Amsterdam's government to quickly and decisively clean up the Bijlmer once and for all.

On 4 October 1992, El Al Flight 1862, a Boeing 747 cargo aircraft, crashed into two of the Bijlmer's residential towers. The plane's three crew members and single passenger died in the incident, as well as a reported 43 people on the ground. However, due to the neighbourhood's large population of undocumented immigrants, it is feared that actual numbers were significantly higher. The catastrophe brought global attention to the Bijlmer's myriad troubles: 'It had a great impact on the Netherlands,' Dekker recalls. 'And it made the government finally focus on resolving the problems of Nassuth's plan.'

This included tearing down almost 60 per cent of the suburb's residential blocks, and significantly reducing the amount of social housing within the development. 'If people have to purchase their home, they feel more responsible,' explains Dekker of the government's gradual implementation of private ownership. 'Because if you ultimately want to sell your apartment, it becomes important to maintain the neighbourhood.'

By this point, Nassuth had already distanced himself from his dream. Increasingly traumatized by the Bijlmer's failure, in 1979 he retired. He and his wife embarked on an extended backpacking trip around the Australian outback, perhaps in a bid to rediscover the freedom of the planner's Dutch East Indies childhood. In 1998, his project was awarded the Oeuvre Prize of the BKVB Foundation. Seven years later, in 2005, Nassuth died.

Learning from the Bijlmer

'The Bijlmer became a game changer for other cities' development,' observes Dekker. Not only did the large-scale experiment swiftly disprove certain tenets of Modernism already being questioned internationally, its failure presented important learnings for a new generation of planners. Nonetheless, the trauma of the Bijlmer project has left Amsterdam cautious, even today. 'Now the city is having to build more new neighbourhoods. Haven-Stad, Amsterdam's port area, slated to accommodate tens of thousands of new homes in the coming years, is a famous example,' explains Dekker. 'But now rather than experiment, they keep it safe. It's become part of Amsterdam's DNA.'

So what went wrong? Nassuth's Bijlmer was flawed on multiple levels, particularly with regard to fragmentation. Key infrastructure was not in place at the time of pioneer tenants moving in to the neighbourhood, leaving them annexed from the rest of the city. And yet, as quickly demonstrated by the rapid disintegration of the Bijlmer's social fabric, the plan relied on an all-or-nothing approach, with no option for a gradual rolling-out of facilities.

Nassuth's plan allowed for zero compromise. Its egalitarian vision did not cater to diversity of requirements or lifestyles, and its sheer scale created a lack of intimacy, and a dearth of opportunities to connect and build community. This led to the isolation of residents, quickly spiralling to social exclusion, exacerbating the discrimination felt by Amsterdam's minority groups forced into the Bijlmer.

For today's planners, clear takeaways from the endeavour include making public transport connections a non-negotiable priority, building flexibility and contingency into plans, and the provision of street life, by way of shops, cafés and entertainment. For Dekker, the failure of the Bijlmer lies as much with Nassuth's idealist ambitions as it does poor management by the city of Amsterdam. 'If you make an experimental neighbourhood it can bring value to your city, but just do it in a small way,' he concludes. 'Start with 1,000 houses, not with a neighbourhood for 100,000 people. That's one of the big mistakes. But it fell to the department of city planning to implement the plan. That's when individual agendas emerged, and ultimately what went wrong with the Bijlmer.'

As the Bijlmer's recent anniversary so colourfully showed, the neighbourhood as it stands today has much to celebrate, with a steady process of transformation gradually but firmly reinserting the once problematic district back into Amsterdam's cultural and social fabric. Nonetheless, for the sake of all cities, its hard-learned lessons must not be forgotten.

Never before have urban residents been better equipped to have an informed opinion on the development of their cities and surroundings. Researcher Menno van der Veen asks how planners can apply new models for urban development in the age of decentralized information and decision-making.

Menno van der Veen/ University of Amsterdam

Participation Matters

'Cities have the capability of providing something for everybody, only because, and only when, they are created by everybody.'[1] Almost sixty years after Jane Jacobs' observation, her statement still sparks debate - particularly with regard to the crucial difference between urban planning *for* all, versus planning *by* all. In the Netherlands, an upcoming amendment to the Environment and Planning Act, or *Omgevingswet*, is nudging this issue further into the spotlight. Although specific details are not yet known, it will impact existing practices of citizen participation and initiatives in the built environment. For this reason, a review of citizen engagement, its benefits, pitfalls, and consequences is timely, according to Menno van der Veen, researcher at the University of Amsterdam and partner at Tertium, a consultancy with a particular focus in spatial planning, local democracy and decision-making.

A decentralized unitary state, the Netherlands' democratic principles have long extended to the structuring and restructuring of its urban environment. In the past 40 years, an increasingly heterogeneous society has seen the country seek ways to facilitate social cohesion and discourage marginalization through *inspraak*, or involvement of the public. Going beyond simply communicating municipalities' plans to community stakeholders, levels of participation may include presenting residents - generally via tenant or neighbourhood organizations - with a choice of built solutions. More involved approaches see local governments engage residents in an advisory capacity, making use of local expertise and insights. Related, many participation schemes in the Netherlands incorporate citizen initiatives, or the deliberate exclusion of certain areas in top-down planning to allow for community-led enterprises: a playground, workshop, or urban farm, for example.

Such participation models can deliver several advantages. In diverse communities in particular, they can encourage inclusiveness; as well as cultivate a sense of ownership, and by extension, responsibility for neighbourhoods. For municipalities and planners, local knowledge can be invaluable in creating suitable solutions for particular areas and groups - particularly when those communities include relevant expertise. After all, *more heads are usually better than one.*

At the time of writing, approaches - and outcomes - of citizen engagement in the Netherlands vary enormously. They depend on factors ranging from individual municipalities' openness, planners' willingness to be flexible, and the organization of communities themselves. It also comes down to residents' expectations, and to a great extent, faith that their concerns or contributions will be considered. However, the New Environment Act, poised to come into force in 2021, will require more projects involve citizen participation - without defining what this means, or in which instances it is an appropriate tool. 'This is why architects should take note of this involvement: while the city is not yet providing definitive answers, this probably will be the future, so it's important to decide what we mean by participation,' urges Van der Veen.

Participation: Why Reciprocity Matters

In the absence of a definitive model for participation in urban development, Van der Veen outlines key considerations for municipalities and planners to facilitate meaningful engagement and make it an integral part of their processes. They include a clear top-down starting point - that is, a defined draft proposal from which to work - as well as identifying stakeholders, clarifying their roles, and establishing a framework for communication.

First and foremost, participation should be thought of as a relational contract, and as such, rooted in trust, transparency, and above all reciprocity. 'It should never be only about governments getting communities' support; it should also be about changing plans because of something the community wants. If there's one party that has nothing to gain from the participation process, then it shouldn't be called that.'

Van der Veen is clear: without reciprocity, meaningful participation cannot exist. Nonetheless, the term is frequently applied to two scenarios in particular that are decidedly *non*-mutual. The first is what Van der Veen describes as consumerism: that is, a straight choice, and usually related to relatively superficial elements of design. Presented with a predefined "this" or "that," the situation may hear residents' opinions, but for the most part, falls short of modifying said solutions in response. As a result, citizens will only be consumers of their environment, and never producers.

'Participation' is also a misnomer when collective or personal politics block exchange - that is, one or both parties' outright refusal to negotiate compromise due to deeply engrained values or beliefs. The proposed development of green belts is particularly susceptible to this form of non-participation: the conviction of residents that these areas should not be built upon leaves no space for negotiation.

Incorporating Culture

How, then, can planners and municipalities avoid these pitfalls, and incorporate meaningful, reciprocal participation into their procedures? First and foremost, developers must identify their target demographics, and if necessary, adapt processes to accommodate local culture. This is essential in facilitating what Van der Veen terms 'project collectivity': 'Every project more or less creates its own collectivity of stakeholders that may work together to forge alliances that otherwise would not have existed.'

Take roads, for example, which may stretch across villages or areas of multiple religious, ethnic, or socio-economic communities. While the bringing together of these groups can bring about long-term positive effects, in the short term it demands municipalities' thoroughness and conscientiousness in identifying spokespeople, registering the interests of a diversity of stakeholders, and most important, designing processes that are inclusive and accessible to all. 'This may mean taking into account things like school holidays or Ramadan, or other customs and obligations that impact residents. As a general rule, planners should have as many seats at the table as possible, ensure a good inventory of interests, and come up with some kind of outcome that tries to do justice to as many interests as possible.'

Role Recognition

A common denominator of recent and ongoing disputes between municipal governments and residents is the attribution and understanding of roles in participatory processes. With no clear guidelines in place, these relational contracts leave considerable scope for misunderstanding, resentment, and conflict.

This occurs on multiple levels, explains Van der Veen. 'Citizen groups are often looked at as just laypersons, even when their residents' association has been in existence for a decade or more, despite their superior knowledge of the local area and its social or environmental issues, and regardless of professional expertise found within groups.' This inevitably causes friction between planners ("let's hear what they have to say and hope they're not too resistant or demanding"), and local communities, who, by virtue of entering into a relational contract, have an expectation to be recognized as advocates, and not 'just' residents.

Illustrating precisely this scenario is an ongoing dispute in Amsterdam's so-called K-buurt ("K- neighbourhood," where all street names start with the letter K) in the Bijlmermeer. The development was pushed into the global spotlight in 1992, when an Israeli airplane crashed into two of its tower blocks. Already dubbed and dismissed as a remote repository for social inequality, the disaster proved the catalyst for the tearing down of most of the Bijlmermeer's buildings. Tower block Kleiburg escaped the razing, and has since become a model for participatory regeneration: in 2017, its residents-remodelled apartments saw the building win both the Mies Van der Rohe Award and the Dutch Design Awards.

Since then however, the relationship between residents, planners, and the municipality has soured. In particular, the opposition of neighbourhood organization, HartvoordeKbuurt (HvdK), to planned redevelopment of a square close to the Kraaiennest metro station has resulted in impasse. The situation is a result of Amsterdam's Zuidoost borough's *institutional* experience of the area's societal problems, versus HvdK's experiential observations. 'Residents are quite adamant,' explains Van der Veen. 'They say, "No! Social policy and physical design are the same thing, so we want an integrated approach. Let's talk about neighbourhood values before making any plan." ' With no clear right or wrong, progress has been on hold for two years.

From both sides, this ongoing dispute boils down to assumptions of roles in the participatory process. For residents, it amounts to a perceived belittling of first-hand experience. From developers' perspective, the local community's unwillingness to engage is seen as a rebuttal of professional insight.

Three Takeaways for Better Participation

Van der Veen proposes several strategies to optimize and facilitate meaningful participation. First and foremost, he encourages municipalities to equip residents with practical tools and resources for discussion and decision making. This may be something as straightforward as a physical space and the provision of suitable refreshments; or it could be the appointment of an external consultant or legal counsel to direct and drive proceedings.

Second, he suggests compensating residents for their input or time - particularly in neighbourhoods where engagement is low. A financial incentive, however token, may help reignite citizens' interest in their local areas.

Finally, he urges the importance of continuous dialogue and ongoing consent, particularly in neighbourhoods without the kind of white-collar professionals for whom contractual processes are a norm (lawyers, architects, and accountants, for example). 'Ongoing consent mechanisms are a key part of the participation process,' explains Van der Veen. 'Without this in place, you risk compelling residents to say yes to a future that they don't understand. The only possible recourse in this scenario is political, which then derails the entire participation process.'

Meaningful participation can and does build better neighbourhoods for communities. In order to succeed, however, planners must be open to flexibility, and take time to understand the interests and concerns of all residents. While it remains to be seen whether any codes of conduct with regard to citizen involvement in planning processes will become statutory requirements in the Netherlands, for inclusive cities of increasingly diverse demographics, participation matters.

The ever-evolving transformative impact of digitalization and hyper-connectivity mean the requirements of our built environments are in a state of constant flux. Here lies potential, argues Berlin-based Marc Schmit of international architecture firm, playze, to build for flexibility and resilience.

Marc Schmit/ playze

Digital Flexibility

In Berlin, adaptability and choice have come to underpin movements and legislation both in terms of how buildings are used, and how people live. However, work-around solutions from all sides have proven either impossible to enforce, or logistically unfeasible. From residents' perspective, they include *Baugruppe*, a model for collective private commissionership of housing, driven by demand for particular housing typologies. However, as groups get increasingly large, their independence from traditional developer models becomes difficult to sustain.

At the same time, and cognisant that new housing developments are beyond the financial means of many, the municipal government has sought to cap rising rents and curtail short-term Airbnb rentals, as well as other similarly difficult-to-enforce regulations. A push-pull struggle with no clear winners, an alternative, more flexible solution to housing is urgently needed for the city to manage growth.

Digitalization can facilitate the adaptability of the built environment, how we navigate cities, and how buildings are used. Extending beyond possibilities for remote working, e-learning, and new forms of recreation, connectivity already actively influences programming. Take the rise and rise of temporary pop-up businesses in unexpected or even hidden locations, for example. Oftentimes promoted exclusively via social media, their success demonstrates how digital tools - in this case, the likes of Instagram, Twitter, as well as mapping and navigation apps - render our cities increasingly fluid, as opposed to fixed, directly impacting how we value space.

By extension, digital tools are also shaping the roles of architects and planners. For Schmit, this is an opportunity to be embraced. Taking Berlin as a starting point, he discusses how online platforms could lend cities around the world new flexibility, enabling and equipping them to respond to the demands of an ever-changing populous.

Berlin: A Casestudy

Although complex, Berlin's rise to one of Europe's biggest cities is far from unique. What's more, like others, the city's housing market currently fails to match a steadily growing population. The Berlin/Brandenburg metropolitan region is currently home to some six million inhabitants, having welcomed in the region of 40,000 annually since 2014. However, at a rate of just 10,000 new units per year, the region's housing supply falls woefully short.

This housing shortfall is most acutely felt in Berlin itself. With around 3.5 million inhabitants, the city's population grew 8.5 per cent between 2010 and 2016, and is projected to exceed 4 million by 2030. Housing aside, other elements of the city's infrastructure are well-equipped to manage this growth: with a polycentric layout, subdivided into 12 districts, Berlin's ring road, highways and *S-bahn* network are long-established. Connections from the centre, to suburbs, and into the Brandenburg countryside are, for the most part, convenient.

The Second World War took a massive toll on Berlin's built environment, with large parts of the city destroyed between 1943 and 1945. After, the sad voids carved out of Berlin took on a new life, providing low-key foundations for temporary, hidden, or in-between businesses. For a time, its temporal state, and an abundance of free space, saw Berlin thrive.

Within the past decade, Berlin's spatial freedom has all but run dry. Almost all available space within the city centre has been bought or sold, and are now the sites of major housing developments. Urbanization has forced increased density, with Alexanderplatz a particularly notable example: no fewer than nine new high-rises have been slated for the area since the 1990s, with plans for Frank Gehry's 150 metre-tall skyscraper currently on hold.[1]

In the west of the once-divided city, too, residential high rises are sprouting apace. And discussions are still ongoing as to how to develop what was once known as a 'death strip' of watch towers along a former stretch of the Berlin Wall, on the banks of the River Spree.

However, these new developments are beyond the financial means of most. With an estimated 800 to 1,400 people vying to rent each "affordable" apartment that comes to market, an uncomfortable fact becomes abundantly clear: Berlin's new housing developments aren't catering to the individuals who most need them: single occupants, and small families.

Three Alternatives to Profit-Driven Developments

Both sides - that is, government and inhabitants - continue to seek ways to counter and contain Berlin's proliferation of profit-driven developments. From residents' perspective, *baugruppe* (literally, 'building group'), is perhaps best known: a community-initiated - and oriented - model for commissioning new housing, it traditionally sees groups of friends directly hire architects to build collective units for several families. A community-focused solution, often with attractive add-ons such as a shared garden, function space, or even sauna, the model started making waves in the early 2000s as an alternative prototype for financing and ownership, as well as better affordability. However, as commissioning groups have grown, so too has risk. In order to accommodate the collective vision of multiple family units, *baugruppe* architects find themselves resorting to a project coordinator, so increasing costs and ultimately reverting to a classic developer model.

Alternative solutions include the syndicated purchasing of existing property, then remodelled for a communal approach to living, and just as important, shared costs. While fruitful in the short-term, these heavily modified properties are rendered all but impossible to then put back on the real estate market.

A third model is that of the cooperative. Although not residential in function, Berlin's Holzmarkt is a successful example of this community-driven initiative.[2] A 12,000sqm project located between Berlin's Ostbahnhof station and the River Spree, the site has been earmarked for development since 2010. When talks between developers and investors collapsed in 2012, the plot was once again put to tender.

A Swiss pension fund swooped in to buy the site, quickly leasing it back to the owners - and regulars - of a legendary bar that until recently, had been the area's principle draw.

The result is a kind of urban village, with community and creativity at its heart. A diverse program of F&B, theatre, workshops, recording studio, artist agency, co-working and more has seen the experiment emerge as one of Berlin's most dynamic neighbourhoods, and a potential model for community-led urban regeneration in other cities.

A Legislative Approach

Berlin's municipal government has also taken steps to ensure the city's expensive new developments stay within the financial means of inhabitants. Although timely - according to a study by property consultancy Knight Frank, prices to buy in Berlin jumped by 20.5 per cent in 2017 alone - in reality, they prove difficult to enforce.[3] Furthermore, with a majority of measures focussed exclusively on the rental market, gaining a foothold on Berlin's property ladder remains an elusive dream for many.

Legislative instruments have included *Zweckentfremdungsverbot*, a law aimed squarely at landlords and apartment owners with a view to banning the misuse of Airbnb. In a nutshell, the measure bans the temporary - and invariably lucrative - renting of properties previously available on the regular, long-term rental market. In theory, the move frees up and makes available the small-sized apartments and houses so in demand in Berlin, for residents as opposed to tourists. In practise, however, it is all but impossible to enforce, and with multiple loopholes.

Second is *Mietpreisbremse*, legislation to cap rising rents. Aimed at applying the brakes on the city's exponentially inflating rental costs, an underpinning factor of Berlin's housing shortage, it prohibits landlords from increasing rents by more than 10 per cent above the local average. To that end, since 2015 the Berlin government has released a two-yearly rental index, the *Mietspiegel* (literally a 'rental mirror') for tenants to check increase claims.[4] However, it has proven to be notoriously difficult to police - not least because with demand for affordable housing significantly outweighing supply, many feel they have little choice but to pay over the odds when apartments do become available.

Compounding the difficulties of enforcing Berlin's rent ceiling are its myriad exceptions, which include certain forms of renovation and modernization. For this reason, recent years have seen Berlin ramp up its *Milieuschutz*, or neighbourhood protection laws. Implemented on a zone by zone basis, it restricts or prohibits landlords from upgrading properties with "luxury" extras: balconies, for example, underfloor heating, guest bathrooms and so on. As well as controlling rent increases, the law is aimed at maintaining communities by preserving social diversity, and reining in rapid gentrification.

A Flexible Solution

Berlin's shortage of affordable housing is far from unique. Like other cities across Europe, its response is to invest heavily in new residential developments. However, Berlin's newest crop of shiny high-rises fail to match the needs and means of its current demographic. The solution, argues Schmit, is a more flexible approach to economic models for real estate. Digitalization already affords us significant flexibility in other areas, from how we communicate and learn, to the ever-expanding shared economy. These shifts already impact how we use, navigate, and understand cities, and will continue to do so. To cater to society's fluctuating housing demands, planners must now incorporate this same flexibility into our built environments.

In recent years, the impact of digitalization has been nothing if not transformative. Practices that seem now commonplace - organizing a Skype call with colleagues abroad, booking an Uber, or shopping online - have quite literally changed how we live and work. More subliminal but no less significant is the impact of everyday online tools that affect how we perceive cities. That includes the birds-eye perspective afforded by Google Maps, through to smart navigation tools that make once hard-to-find locations readily accessible. 'There's a revaluation of the city through those tools,' observes Schmit. 'That has a great impact when we start discussing values of land within the city.' The trend for pop-up restaurants presents a prime example of precisely this phenomenon: an expensive, central location is no longer a prerequisite for success; shareability and communication are.

Fashion aside, the appetite for pop-up eateries, bars or stores can also be said to be reflective of risk. After all, temporary spaces, low running costs, and moveable operations make considerable sense in today's volatile economic climate. The shift extends to architecture, with architects increasingly being challenged to design not just for multipurpose programming, but public spaces with the potential to be reprogrammed time and time again. 'Right now, we're seeing lots of temporary, small structures happening in urban contexts, but also longterm constructions which need a highly flexible and adaptive design,' observes Schmit. New typologies tailored to contemporary needs, the trend is particularly visible in the rise and rise of "exhibition" or "cultural" venues and spaces - as opposed to the more concrete and fixed museum model.

Taking the concept of flexible spaces several steps further is a recent trend for modular hotels, operating on a supply-and-demand basis. Via a dedicated app, users can request accommodation for particular destinations, or track the location of the hotel's mobile units. Comprising multiple shipping containers, the idea is that accommodations expand or shrink - or relocate entirely - according to user demand.

Against this backdrop of building for flexibility is the contemporaneous emergence of "Prop-Tech": digital platforms aimed at disrupting the traditional property market, including new economic models for real estate. Right now, the sector spans everything from blockchain, to using artificial intelligence and virtual reality technologies as a means to view properties remotely.

Could an amalgamation of existing forms of flexibility already visible in new architectural requirements, and incorporating qualities of our shared economy, combined with a PropTech approach, create new economic models for tenants in cities like Berlin? Without question, the need is there: in today's rapidly changing sociopolitical environment, fuelled in part by digitally driven globalization, as well as an unstoppable trend towards urbanization, the longterm provision of adequate, affordable housing emerges as an urgent issue for cities worldwide.

The housing of a society in flux, argues Schmit, calls for flexibility. His vision combines digital planning processes with user-sourced requirements. Building on a base structure that incorporates the social functions of community living - a shared garden, for example, bar, electric vehicles or even childcare facilities - prospective tenants submit their accommodation requirements via an online platform, according to their current needs. Moveable, stackable units, making use of pre-fabricated elements, can be then added or subtracted according to demand, thereby creating communities that work for *now*.

The solution allows for not just flexibility of price, but also customization and choice of features during the digital planning process. Calling for a radical rethink of architects' role, Schmit acknowledges, 'The requirements of architecture get reduced to absolute minimum if spaces stay flexible enough.'

The Fluid Approach

Planning for the kind of social unpredictability felt by nations around the world is a challenge to which architects and planners have no choice but to rise. In Berlin, residents and lawmakers continue to seek to mitigate the impact of a housing shortfall through community-based alternatives to unaffordable models, as well as implementing rent caps. However, these solutions are fast proving to be either unsustainable, or else impossible to enforce. For this reason, planners must now expand their horizons, make flexible their role, and above all, unshackle their industry from traditional models. This calls for increased incorporation of digital instruments and tools, as well as an adaptable, more fluid approach that moves with - not against - the fluctuating needs of cities, and the residents who live there.

Technology will change the way we work in a dramatic way. This has enormous implications for the role of the office within urbanism. If work becomes a lifestyle instead of a necessity, we need to dramatically rethink the function of work in our cities, says architect Florian Idenburg.

Florian Idenburg/ SO-IL

The Future of Work

From densification and building new infrastructure, to accommodating growth and preserving green spaces, the city of Amsterdam is planning for its future. The city government's recently released Structural Vision 2040 outlines a series of wide-ranging expansions, including new homes and the creation of between 45,000 and 58,000 new jobs in the future district of Haven-Stad.[1] But as technology continues to shape the world of work, how can city builders of today prepare for the labour landscape of tomorrow? To compare the work ideologies, economies, and tools of just 50 years ago to those of now reveals staggering change. Looking ahead, there is every reason to believe that the environment will continue to evolve, both in ways we can predict - artificial intelligence, robots, and telecommuting, for example - as well as ways in which we cannot. These unknowns also spell change for architects: 'It means we won't design for function anymore,' reckons Florian Idenburg, co-founder of New York-based architecture and design firm, SO-IL. 'For cities, this will translate to providing a diversity of environments in which to work, rather than a diversity of functions. I think it will be less about space planning, and more about creating spaces that can evoke insights.'

In reviewing spaces of productivity of the past 50 years in the United States, including suburban campuses, remote laboratories, as well as government buildings, Idenburg identifies a rich history of, as he calls it, 'architecture of good intentions.' But as society - including technology, economies, politics, and trends - typically moves faster than architecture is able, many of these once visionary work spaces quickly became obsolete. As such, they deliver valuable learnings to today's professionals: firstly, that the function of buildings is susceptible to rapid and dramatic change from all spheres. As a consequence, therefore, creating flexible spaces that are able to bend to future priorities and ideologies is a smart strategy in thinking about tomorrow's cities.

Architects and Work

Falling somewhere in-between the realms of private and public, the work space is traditionally associated less with "architecture," and more with interior design. Indeed, this was a starting point for SO-IL's research, and in 2017, the practice worked with office furniture and systems firm, Knoll, to create a series of conceptual hybrid objects titled Future Work. 'They asked us, "What sort of furniture will we need when no one sits at a desk anymore?" This got us thinking beyond chairs and desks, and to what that future might look like in a broader sense. If robots assume a more prominent position in the workplace, what will replace it?'

The project led to a series of research and design studios at Harvard Graduate School of Design examining a range of architectural precedents in terms of US workspaces. Together, they reveal fascinating correlations between particular eras' cultural movements and their respective work environments, and in doing so, raise important questions and considerations for not only architects, but also policy makers, economists, and businesses of all kinds.

First, how might architects extrapolate this established symbiotic relationship between societal values and offices to create new prototype work spaces? And if robots and computers are to continue to replace human labour, what alternative activities might we develop to compensate, both in terms of the fulfilment and sense of purpose work can provide, as well as financial? This issue also has political and economic bearings: as robotization renders full-time employment within certain industries or at particular levels economically unviable for employers, how might new welfare systems such as universal basic income on the one hand support society, as well as liberate it from menial work?

At the same time, technology is already facilitating the so-called “gig economy” in industries spanning everything from content production and coding, through to transportation and translation. If more and more of us are able to, choose to, or are forced to work independently, will large-sized corporate offices become a thing of the past, and simply not worth the financial outlay? From a societal perspective, these lone workers - be they freelancers or independent contractors - are on the one hand afforded great freedoms, but may also risk becoming disengaged and detached from people and purpose. This has already prompted the rise of co-working spaces in cities around the world.

In Europe and the US, today’s work landscape is radically different from that of 50 years ago. But to look at its physicality - be it the contemporary proliferation of co-working spaces, gender-neutral bathrooms in office buildings, not to mention standing desks - shows that just as before, culture and society are key shapers of workspace architecture.

A Shifting Corporate Culture

This tendency is evidenced from as early as the beginning of the twentieth century, with Frank Lloyd Wright's five-storey high red brick building for the Larkin Soap Company in New York. A classic example of a Taylorist workspace - that is, a setting for order, hierarchy, seamless synchrony and structure - it quite literally promoted its values to workers by way of panels of wall inscriptions depicting qualities such as 'sacrifice,' 'control,' 'cooperation,' 'economy,' and 'industry.' In this building, as well as Lloyd Wright's later headquarters for Johnson Wax, entrenched class divides of the time were reflected in the architect's over-arching influence on everything from pen holders to chairs, and in particular, the buildings' layout: workers were positioned on the ground floor, with bosses situated above to monitor productivity. 'This was the predominant way of planning,' explains Idenburg. 'The organization of the workspace resembled the organization of the company, so where you found yourself in the office was also where you found yourself in the company. This led to tensions because employees lacked individual agency; they were literally subject to an overarching corporate structure.'

Fast forward to the 1950s, and the sense of freedom in the aftermath of two devastating world wars was acutely felt in the workplace. In Europe, widespread reconstruction and rapid economic growth met with a recently tested and renewed sense of egalitarianism, resulting in an entirely new approach to office design: *Bürolandschaft*, or "office landscape" was devised by a German consulting group in 1958. Focused on individualism while encouraging participation, it incorporated private cubicles with organic spatial groupings for collaborative work, breaking down the hierarchies of its more linear predecessors.

This trend for semi-open workspaces arrived in the US soon after. Herman Miller's Action Office line was especially influential in organizing office furniture for a balance of collaboration and privacy, which contrasted starkly with the open rows of traditional desks that came before. Further breaking up the formerly staid, anonymous office spaces of previous decades was the introduction of nature into work, best evidenced by Kevin Roche's Ford Foundation Building in New York. Completed in 1968, its tree-filled atrium marked a first for the city, and was a precursor to offices and companies leaving the stresses, complications, and soaring costs of cities behind for suburban locations.

By the early 1970s, counterculture and playfulness were permeating discussions around architecture and work. This was driven in part the likes of Constant Nieuwenhuys with his New Babylon project; or British architect Cedric Price, whose Fun Palace event/spaces started to introduce notions of leisure and play. Where these artists/architects explored leisure as anti-work, their insights in human behaviour were gradually absorbed within work culture. One can argue they were a forerunner to today's SXSW-type creative-cum-professional conferences and festivals.

Around the same time, iconic and alternative media images of a new breed of enigmatic, guru-esque type of "company man" in unexpected workplaces - Hugh Hefner in bed in the Playboy Mansion, for example - further disrupted and subverted traditional office work concepts. Toppling stereotypes in other arenas, and an extension of the civil rights movement of the previous decade, women were also rising up workforce ranks - and beyond the traditional typing pool shackles. In 1970, the Women's Strike for Equality marked the fiftieth anniversary of the passage of the Nineteenth Amendment to the US Constitution, which gave women the right to vote.

The Role of Technology

According to Idenburg, technology has been the biggest driver of change in the workplace over the past century, with the mobility the internet affords playing a key role in architecture. Extending beyond simply *what* computers can do, this also relates to their physicality: during the 1940s, 1950s, and 1960s, colossal calculating machines and telephone exchanges measuring tens of metres in length called for significant space. Since the turn of the twenty-first century in particular, our office tech has become smaller, more portable, and with increased functionality. As a result, workplace architectural requirements have become similarly simplified and streamlined. After all, in a paperless office, why make space for archives?

Of course, the influence of technology extends far beyond the size and layout of buildings. The communication, flexibility, and independence today's tech tools allow have not only shaped organizational structure, but also presented big corporations with an attractive new model to emulate: the freer, more egalitarian working styles of young tech start-up companies. A flattening-out of organizational structures - that is, a dismantling of hierarchy through the removal or consolidation of mid-level supervisory or managerial divides - is reflected in workspaces themselves. More open plan and often incorporating hot desks as opposed to fixed, they are far removed from those highly hierarchical spaces of the first decade of the 1900s that positioned watchful bosses in galleries and glass boxes above - and away from - the work floor.

'Maybe technology has taken over hierarchy and organization,' suggests Idenburg. 'That means as architects, we're liberated from having to think about things like corner offices and translating corporate systems into plans. Instead, we have scope to think about what we could build to open up the imagination of a worker.'

Work and Play?

In recent years, technology has blurred the formerly rigid boundaries that once separated work from other areas of our lives. Thanks to laptop computers and smartphones, for example, anywhere from the coffeeshop, to the beach, to the home is every bit as legitimate a workplace as a dedicated office. Similarly, these same tools make traditional working hours - nine to five, say - meaningless, particularly in a globalized world of partnerships and collaborations spanning multiple time zones. For better or worse, work and life are no longer separated.

This modern reality is evidenced and enabled in workplace architecture through elements focused on wellbeing, relaxation, and play: an office today is just as required to have a foosball table, for example, as it is to have a meeting room. Fittingly, it is the tech companies themselves driving this trend, and Google's Googleplex campus in Mountain View, California, famously boasts EnergyPods for employees to take naps during their working day.[2]

Interestingly, this contemporary blurring of work, leisure, and play in terms of office planning is increasingly reinforced in companies' culture. Enterprise gamification, for example, is being employed more and more for training, motivation, and engagement.

The Future of Work Architecture

Today's work landscape is virtually unrecognizable from that of just 50 years ago. Now seamlessly integrated into a more holistic contemporary understanding of life and lifestyle, it has been *de*compartmentalized in every sense - including architecture. Furthermore, if technology continues its steady march towards robotics and automation, it seems likely that productivity will become yet more closely aligned with lifestyle and choice. That is, should a human workforce become economically unviable, what options will we have for replacing the fulfilment, sense of belonging, education, and mental exercise work provides?

Based on current trends, as well as speculation as to what the future may bring, Idenburg proposes several possible scenarios. A "Work Spa," for example, could be a space blending physical health and wellbeing with possibilities for personal betterment through education. Or, will further saturation of the "gig economy" and the increasing ease of remote working motivate people to escape city life and deurbanize for a freer existence? Similarly feasible, will the legal risk associated with today's more egalitarian, socio-democratic work environment - particularly with regard to gender and discrimination - dissuade corporations from maintaining fixed locations within national jurisdictions? Could mobile workspaces, perhaps moving around international waters and with drone-powered internet, offer practical solutions for firms unwilling or unable to abide by new laws?

Already understood as a shaper of human behaviour and societal driver, architecture most certainly has a role to play in the future of work. That may be through new buildings, or it may be through planning and design to provoke, challenge, or prompt regulation. Regardless of specifics, on a fundamental level, it calls for a futurist outlook, and by extension, flexibility. With this in mind, Idenburg proposes an important short-term response for a new generation of architects: 'We need to stop thinking of the office as something functional in the Modernist sense, but of a place where people come together to achieve something, within a certain, temporary context or dynamic framework.'

Cities are not only relying on top-down planned traffic infrastructures, but also on the many informal and flexible systems that are as important. Understanding and experimenting with these forms of infrastructures is critical. The city of the future needs to facilitate and exploit these kinds of infrastructures, argue Selva Gürdoğan and Gregers Tang Thomsen.

Selva Gürdoğan & Greger Thomsen/ Superpool

Flexible Systems

'Community building is one of the most urgent things we have to do.' So says Gregers Tang Thomsen who along with Selva Gürdoğan co-founded Istanbul-based multidisciplinary design studio, Superpool. Underlining the practice's approach, the statement also alludes to dual side effects of a top-down approach to city-building.

On the one hand, the strategy can stamp out decades-old informal structures - both physical and societal - that lend cities their character and spirit. Yet at the same time, heavy-handed formalization can also be a catalyst for innovative workaround fixes at a grassroots level. These can address infill gaps or otherwise compensate for shortcomings of official solutions. By closely examining the imperfections of top-down urban planning, as well as the ad hoc and community-driven improvization they can stimulate, a new generation of city builders can integrate these findings into a more efficient, more inclusive model for future development. This calls for a research-based strategy, a seeking out of alternative viewpoints, and new ways of mapping.

Urban planning has never been so urgent as it is now. According the UN's Department of Economic and Social Affairs, 55 per cent of the world's population now live in urban areas. By 2050, an additional 2.5 billion people will take this figure to 68 per cent.[1] In order to manage current growth of existing populaces, as well as prepare for an inevitable influx, cities are investing in densification and mobility. In many countries, it seems, the cost, construction, and scale associated with this necessary infrastructure - which includes housing developments and new public transport - can only be realized by government-led, top-down planning.

But in developing economies in particular, urgency forces simplistic solutions that are fast found wanting. Take current modes of housing development, for example. When mismanaged, these do not only result in homogeneity, but also erode social cohesion through a physical failure to accommodate the very exchange and exposure that sparks culture. At one end they include quickly erected towers delivering low-cost accommodation at cities' affordable and merely available, peripheries. At the other are gated communities, generally pitched at a higher price point and similarly removed from central downtown areas. Increasingly widespread in cities globally, these distinct and disparate approaches first and foremost segregate people, drive class divides, and cleave communities apart.

Downtown, the effects of market-driven approaches to planning are first felt on the street, where real estate development drives gentrification to shape public spaces. But as street food vendors are moved on, informal wet markets shut down, or impromptu play areas limited, so too are the informal economies. These informal markets don't just lend cities their identity and character, they also provide work and opportunities that heavy-handed or knee-jerk planning fails to take into account.

A current strategy of raze, rebuild, and rehouse

deprives all inhabitants of cultural richness, nuance, and choice. To better serve communities, uphold efficiency, and foster entrepreneurship, cities must find ways to accommodate and harness existing bottom-up initiatives and economies. Flexibility is essential for preserving - and indeed, *prompting* - grass-roots actions and infrastructure in otherwise top-down environments. Furthermore, an inbuilt ability to adapt and absorb change bolsters cities' resilience to those events for which it cannot plan. These could be yet-unimagined technologies, for example; or as has been the case in Istanbul, the repercussions of regional conflict.

Istanbul: Growth and Change

Now with a population in excess of 15 million, Istanbul has long been one of the world's most populous cities. However, the second half of the twentieth century proved transformative, as mass rural to urban migration from Eastern Turkey saw numbers swell from around a million people in 1950, to a staggering 8.8 million in 2000. Ever since, the population has continued to grow.

The twenty-first century has brought further change to the transcontinental city. With a steady population growth of 3.45 per cent, its economic rise is well-documented.[2] According to a 2017 report by the Turkish Statistical Institute, Istanbul's share in the country's GDP was 31.2 per cent.[3] The city's wealth is evidenced by recent years' impressive infrastructure projects (the submarine Marmaray Tunnel, for example, linking Europe and Asia underneath the Bosporus strait); a proliferation of luxury hotels; and burgeoning cultural sector.

At the same time, an expanding middle class has caused

an exponential increase in private vehicle ownership. In addition to raised levels of air pollution, a direct repercussion is Istanbul's now notorious congestion: In TomTom's most recent Traffic Index, the city ranks as the world's sixth-most congested.[4] In January 2019, mayoral candidate and former Prime Minister, Binali Yıldırım, told journalists, 'We have asked [people] what the biggest problem in Istanbul is... Without any exceptions, residents in all districts say it is transportation and traffic.'[5]

In the past few years, political unrest has propelled Turkey to international consciousness. In 2013, a sit-in at Istanbul's Taksim Gezi Park, initially protesting planned urban development of the area, sparked a wave of demonstrations and violence across the country, the likes of which had not been seen since the 1970s.[6] Although multifaceted, core issues were freedom of speech, and the policies of current President Recep Tayyip Erdoğan.

Further focusing the international spotlight onto Turkey, and a significant driver of change in Istanbul, has been the ripple effect of the conflict in Syria. An inadvertent stage for the repercussions of war, Turkey has become a way point for refugees. According to US-based nonprofit public policy organization, The Brookings Institution, in 2018 there were more than 560,000 registered Syrian refugees in Istanbul, with over 50,000 living in the single district of Zeytinburnu.[7]

For Superpool, all of these developments, traumas, and events shape Istanbul, and as such, present useful insights for creating a new urban landscape to accommodate change. 'In terms of mapping Istanbul, and especially its public space, we needed to evolve from looking at the city in terms of data, numbers and lines into being more engaged with the politics of the place,' explains Gürdoğan. Doing so reveals grass-root, bottom-up and above all, people-led systems - activism included - that planners must take into consideration in implementing urban upgrades that are democratic, efficient, and inclusive.

Mobility Matters

Superpool's research focus in mapping the gaps that result from societal change and shortcomings of formalization began in 2006, when Gürdoğan and Thomsen first relocated to Istanbul. 'It was long before we all had iPhones in our pockets and instant access to GPS,' recalls Gürdoğan. 'We had to learn the city, how to navigate it.'

This was the background to the self-initiated project, Dolmuş & Minibüs Map. Both forms of shared public transportation in Istanbul, *dolmuş* first emerged during the 1940s. Effectively communal taxis, today, they largely ferry people to, from or between officially designated public transport stops. However, unlike formalized infrastructure, drivers determine their own routes according to demand, traffic, and personal schedule. Although similar to *dolmuş*, the *minibüs* system is associated more with peripheral suburbs, and as such, lower-income passengers. Both indicative of Istanbul's predilection for improvisation, the systems' existence highlights shortcomings of official networks, particularly with regard to efficiency and cost, and a clear need of inhabitants.

'What's curious about this system is that, of course, it functions perfectly without a map because it's all based on communication,' explains Thomsen. As such, it presents a prime example of blended top-down and bottom-up infrastructures whose purpose, function, and demand is clear.

Opening Walls

Elsewhere, the studio has looked to ways post-urban development could compensate for specific shortcomings of Istanbul's most prevalent housing typology: repetitive clustered towers, inside enclosed and gated perimeters, commonly located far from the city centre. Largely instigated and managed by the Housing Development Agency of Turkey (Toplu Konut İdaresi Baİkanlıİı, or TOKI), estates' remoteness from downtown services, as well as their physical isolation, reduces social interaction and results in a lack of employment possibilities. In every sense, these modern developments are far, far removed from the improvised infrastructures - street vendors, wet markets and bazaars, for example - that have forged Istanbul's historic identity.

'We thought about how to reintroduce informality to formality. Both state housing and fancier private developments, they all do offer some amenities - schools and sports facilities, for example - but are still lacking. We wanted to offer a reaction to what was missing,' explains Gürdoğan.

With this in mind, and in partnership with Paris-based Atelier d'Architecture Autogérée,[8] Superpool launched KITO (Kolektif İşbirlikçi Toplum Oluşumu, The Collective and Collaborative Agency). The project is primarily aimed at retrofitting Istanbul's concrete outposts with some of the city's signature bottom-up improvisation and entrepreneurship. Far from a simple indulgence of nostalgia, their conceptual interventions are designed to transform suburbs. In particular, the facilitation of small businesses and programming along estates' boundary perimeters - or "wall shops" - may help to recreate some of the social interactions otherwise lost through decentralization. 'It's about reoccupying the borders between compounds,' explains Thomsen.

Future Citizens

In keeping with Superpool's commitment to assessing cities from alternative and overlooked viewpoints, the studio has recently embarked on Istanbul95. Their contribution to this project aims at optimizing cities for learning and development through play during early childhood. A collaboration with The Bernard van Leer Foundation's Urban95 initiative, it surveys the city from an elevation of 95 centimetres - the average height of a 3 year old.[9]

In Istanbul and elsewhere, public spaces are the first to succumb to privatization. Yet for city dwellers, parks and squares present a formative first playground for children and babies. In this way, current strategies fail to take into account the wellbeing of cities' youngest residents.

A very literal meeting of top-down and bottom-up, the project calls on policy makers and municipalities to review and prioritize play areas and accessibility for children. As a result, four pilot neighbourhood playgrounds are scheduled for completion in Istanbul in 2019.

Engagement

'In our first three years in Istanbul, we saw ourselves as outsiders, looking at the city as if from a satellite but not really on the ground,' Thomsen recalls. 'But to really impact the future of a city, you can't just be floating on top: you need be politically engaged with its actors.'

Such engagement reveals the myriad grass-roots activations and infrastructures that lend cities their unique characters and identity. Moreover, their existence points to functions and needs that in the case of Istanbul, and elsewhere, are invariably overlooked in the rolling-out of city plans and gentrification. By preserving and promoting metropolises' flexibility and historic ability to absorb change, cities can be more resilient, and better equipped to handle transformations both predicted, as well as spontaneous. The most dynamic, exciting and vibrant cities globally see top-down systems accommodate bottom-up infrastructures: for sustainable communities and long-term success, a new generation must plan accordingly.

An ever-evolving information technology sector will play an important role in planning the public services in the city of the future. We need to exploit these options to improve cities, says Valerie von der Tann.

Valerie von der Tann/ ViaVan

Smart Cities

'The most important thing smart cities should do is improve quality of life for citizens, residents, and people. It's not about the technology, but about how we are using it.' Described in this way, Valerie von der Tann's vision for smart cities echoes the values urban planners place on the built environment. By combining the insight, ideas, and skill sets of both smart specialists and planners, she argues, we can improve cities' efficiency and liveability for improved quality of life.

Since the term's emergence in around 2008, public understanding of "smart city" concepts have been manifold and evolutionary, thanks in part to a formative period of trial and error. Initially met with cynicism, technology firms' early willingness to engage with city governments was seen as little more than a marketing strategy. The concept also carries connotations of distrust, and fear of a dystopian future chained to technology. Others take the opposite view: that a digital path can rid us of all society's problems. Further adding to the confusion, in recent years' planning parlance, "smart city" has been overused to the extent of becoming a nebulous buzz word, employed to convey modernity, resilience and forward-thinking.

For Von der Tann, all of the above readings miss the purpose, point, and potential of what a smart city should be. 'It's a city in which different actors use digital technology to solve public problems and improve quality of life. Smart cities are only really smart if technology is being put to work to achieve positive impact.' A co-author of McKinsey Global Institute's 2018 report, *Smart Cities: Digital Solutions for a More Liveable Future*, she evidences instances around the world where the implementation of an expanding toolkit of digital applications are changing residents' life for the better. To measure impact, the report defines seven dimensions of overall quality-of-life, spanning everything from health and safety, to time and convenience.

For urban planners, a key takeaway of McKinsey's research is that when it comes to upgrading cities to smart status, one size does not fit all. Rather, successful implementation of specific applications depends on several factors, including existing infrastructure. When done right, quality-of-life indicators show improvement of up to 30 per cent which translates to tangible reductions in everything from maternal mortality rates to commuting time. In order to optimize cities' efficiency, then, particularly with regard to public services, planners must incorporate smart city digital applications into built environments. Technology is driving change in cities and society; the methods, approaches and targets of planners must respond accordingly.

Defining Smart Cities

Smart cities use technology to either directly improve residents' quality of life, or transmit specific data to enable better decision-making. For this to happen requires three layers of activation. The first is a technology base, by way of sensors and a critical mass of devices - smartphones, for example - adequately connected by high-speed broadband. The second is an application designed to translate received data to useful, actionable output. Third is the adopting of these systems by people or governments.

To illustrate these criteria, Von der Tann cites an increasingly common mode of transport in cities globally: an e-hailing app, like Uber, Lyft or Didi. In this instance, smartphones serve as a sensor to transmit users' demand and location. The application's algorithm relays this data to drivers, using both parties' positions and cars' availability to create matches. The process is completed on drivers and users successfully meeting, ie, an in-person transaction.

The e-hailing model presents a straightforward example of smart city infrastructures that will be familiar to many. Nevertheless, despite widespread adoption of specific, individual components, the smart city concept is still contested. Opposition stems in part from public distrust of technology companies and how governments use data. Elsewhere, the potential of smart cities has been misunderstood and exaggerated to the point of distortion, either envisioned as creating technology dystopias, or else ridding society of all of its troubles. 'In my opinion, the challenge now is to create optimistic but realistic understandings of the potential of technology that is there in urban settings and be smart about how to use it in an inclusive, equitable, effective way,' explains Von der Tann.

The Very Public Evolution of the Smart City Concept

Part of the confusion surrounding smart cities lies in the idea's tumultuous history. 'The active period of smart city started around 2008,' explains Von der Tann.

'Because much of the initial hype was driven by technology companies, many took the cynical view that these firms were trying to ride out the concurrent financial crisis by looking to governments and cities as an alternative and stable customer base.'

IBM was an early driver of international smart city projects. However, an ambitious data centre in Rio de Janeiro ultimately had a negative effect on the concept's uptake. In 2010, one year after the city was declared host of the 2016 Summer Olympics, IBM's somewhat ominously named Integrated Center of Command and Control was officially inaugurated. But if the scale of the project was impressive - it brought together 30 municipal departments and private service providers, tracking everything from traffic and meteorology, to emergency services - its Orwellian image proved damaging. A 2014 report in *The Guardian* described the nerve centre as a, 'Nineteen Eighty-Four-style vision already alarmingly realised. It is festooned with screens like a NASA Mission Control for the city.'[1]

Nonetheless, others followed Rio's lead: in 2010 the EU declared smart cities a priority for the Europe 2020 strategy; and by 2012, China had announced a list of 90 pilot smart cities for future investment.[2] But the initial momentum didn't create enough meaningful results for citizens, a fact which further fuelled the notoriety surrounding smart cities. 'City governments were trying to establish themselves as high-tech and cutting-edge. A few chose solutions before really understanding the problems. Others may have increased efficiency somewhere, but didn't really solve issues for citizens on the ground,' explains Von der Tann.

Around the same time, several seminal publications further compounded the poor public image of smart cities. Contributing to the growing sense of disillusionment, *The Economist* hosted an influential online debate, titled 'Are Smart Cities Empty Hype?' Certainly, it was looking that way.

'All of these concerns and discussions were so important, because they allowed the concept to evolve, which in recent years has led to renewed optimism,' asserts Von der Tann. A particular shift has been that of scale: smart city activations are no longer the preserve of huge technology companies and governments. Indeed, as Von der Tann's ride-sharing example demonstrates, its actors today are just as likely to be start-ups and private consumers, operating on a city-to-city basis. 'Smart cities evolved from one-size-fits-all technology solutions to being about continuous innovation that is constantly adjusted to specific local contexts,' summarizes Von der Tann.

The Current Landscape of Smart Cities

For its recent research, McKinsey Global Institute measured the impact of a range of digital applications in cities globally. It found they are already alleviating particular public problems by 10 to 30 per cent. It also found that success rates of specific applications depend significantly on city's underlying characteristics and existing infrastructure. Moreover, for governments and planners, smart city solutions should be combined with other tools - governance and building, for example - to optimize efficiency and quality of life.

Von der Tann explains, '[Smart city applications] aren't

able to entirely solve problems like safety or long commute times by themselves, but they can certainly offer substantial incremental improvements. And these are solutions that require less investment than training new doctors, for example, or building new roads. So what they can do is optimize what's already here in terms of infrastructure, both physical and human.'

An initial challenge was to define what quantifies quality of life in the context of cities. For its study, McKinsey settled on seven categories that collectively address practical as well as emotional concerns of city living, and importantly, can be measured. The dimensions are Safety; Time and Convenience; Health; Environment; Social Connectedness; Jobs; and Cost of Living. Researchers then analysed how a set of existing digital applications are currently impacting change in 50 cities worldwide.

Take time and convenience: For many, this translates to the daily commute, which globally averages at over one hour each day. The research revealed that the impact of different application types - be they e-hailing solutions such as Uber or Lyft, intelligent traffic systems, or smart phone apps delivering real-time public transport information - varies considerably from city to city, depending on how existing infrastructure has shaped commuters' daily habits.

In New York, for example, where more than half of workers travel by subway, real-time public transport apps recorded savings of 8 per cent - or six to seven minutes - among those using this commute method. But in Rio, where most travel either by bus or private vehicle, due in part to the city's comparatively weak subway system, intelligent traffic systems were shown to be the most impactful of surveyed commute-related digital applications, accounting for average reductions of 5 per cent, or four minutes. The second most efficient smart application in the Brazilian city was digital tickets and payment solutions, resulting in a 2 per cent - or two minute - reduction in commute time. 'So smart cities aren't one-size-fits-all. The impact of individual applications very much differs according to the city you're looking at,' says Von der Tann.

Interestingly, certain digital applications ostensibly aimed at tackling a particular type of city problem show greater impact in other areas. For example, according to the study, congestion zone pricing in cities such as London would neither positively or negatively influence commute times. While it decreases average commute time for the people on the road, it increases the commute for those being priced off the road. 'But it does have a positive effect in reducing noise and pollution,' says Von der Tann. Similarly, e-hailing applications have in many situations been shown to increase the number of cars on the road, and therefore not to improve commute time. But from a safety perspective, their influence is significant because they offer a convenient, easy alternative to driving tired or drunk.

Smart city solutions also show considerable potential in the field of health, with average improvements of between 8 to 15 per cent. In the context of London's high rate of chronic illness and lifestyle diseases, the most impactful is remote patient monitoring. A proactive and preventive approach to treating chronic conditions, patients read their vital signs at home and send direct to their doctor. Only if the medical practitioner has concerns do patients go to hospital, thus relieving some of the burden on cities' healthcare facilities. 'For elderly people who want to live at home, the power of these applications should not be underestimated,' notes Von der Tann.

Lifestyle and healthcare wearables also show promise. Looking beyond their current application as primarily exercise trackers, they could also be used to monitor diabetes, for example, or support smoking cessation. 'This is especially important because to look at global urban development, we see middle income cities rapidly taking on the chronic lifestyle diseases more commonly associated with high income cities.' At a point in time where China is poised to soon equal the diabetes rate of the US, such smart interventions must become an urgent priority.

Smart city applications can also boost cities' safety. Tools such as predictive police monitoring, for example, make for better decision-making in terms of where to deploy personnel, resulting in a 30 to 40 per cent reduction in criminal incidents in some cities. Elsewhere, and in the face of exponentially rising rates of urbanization, industrialization, and consumption globally, smart solutions also present means of mitigating cities' environmental impact. Particularly pertinent in economies including China and India, applications such as dynamic electricity pricing can reduce greenhouse gas emissions by 10 to 15 per cent, cut unrecycled waste by 15 to 20 per cent through digital waste tracking, and reduce water consumption by 20 to 30 percent by way of leakage detection.

The Outlook for Smart Cities

'If we get this right, I think smart cities will not be a dystopia, but deeply human spaces with a quality of life enhanced by technology,' concludes Von der Tann.

McKinsey's research underlines the vast potential of deploying smart city solutions to complement alternative and existing infrastructures. But what does a smart city look like? According to the report, the five cities with the highest rollout of smart applications currently are New York City, Los Angeles, London, Seoul and in particular, Singapore. All share similar strengths - notably in the fields of security, utilities, healthcare, and economic development - and all are high income. But more important, Von der Tann explains, is having the technology to collect information; a strong broadband network; and in particular, open data platforms: 'We can have data out there, but if it's not accessible to the developer community who want to build something then it doesn't do much.'

Von der Tann sees smart solutions as an important component in a holistic approach to urban development that blends legislative, community-based, physical, and digital elements. 'City governments should refresh their approach to infrastructure provisioning to combine both physical and smart means for optimal impact. To be successful, this needs to be done in a way that promotes equitable access and also addresses community concerns around privacy.'

A core tenet of the vision that the McKinsey Global Institute presents is placing people first. Beyond identifying cities' problems and challenges through public engagement, this also extends to locating and fostering specific skill sets that historically have not been linked to city planning. 'Governments should create latitude across agencies, and incorporate civic talent to develop these expertise.' In upgrading cities, urban planners must similarly expand their remit to include rapidly developing digital tools.

Acknowledging the shift in scope of planners smart cities requires, Von der Tann concludes, 'In the past, there's been a sharp divide between technologists and urbanists. Now it's time to combine knowledge for productive ways to shape urban environments in directions that encourage that and make the most positive use of technology.'

To stop the growth of so-called "grey zones" on urban fringes, architect Neville Mars calls for a radical approach: extreme densification of current metropolitan areas, and a renewed focus on injecting innovation into the countryside.

Neville Mars/ MARS Architects

The Grey Zone

The implications of urbanization are becoming increasingly visible around the globe. According to the most recent projections released by the UN, some 68 per cent of the world's population will live in cities by 2050.[1] On a societal level, this ongoing migration could suggest increased mobility and wealth, as well as higher standards of living. But on an environmental level, the results could be devastating.

All over the world, the physical borders of cities are expanding. The growing urban footprint is partnered with the simultaneous relocation of traditionally urban facilities and functions - manufacturing, for example - into peripheral areas to make way for residential developments. As a result, so-called "grey zones" emerge between cities, landing oftentimes polluting industries into formerly rural areas. Over time, these areas expand to accommodate other forms of urban overspill, including housing. Poorly planned and poorly regulated, the grey zones expand and amalgamate, eating into the countryside.

The nebulous nature of grey zone development makes it a particularly definition-resistant phenomenon. Certainly for rapidly growing economies, practical and scientific answers are extremely hard to formulate. Instead, recent years have seen planners and policymakers respond to ambitions for sustainable urban growth with an expanding new lexicon of buzzwords: "Smart City," "Sponge City," "Creative City," and so on. Invariably reliant on new technologies, such plans ignore the reality of the grey zone, and instead simply project more greenfield projects amidst its muddied landscapes.

The problem: they fail to assert what has now become an urgent non-negotiable. Without a sustainable planning model that avoids the proliferation of the grey zone, we should not plan there. For architect and urban planner, Neville Mars, this calls for an uncompromising parallel focus: extreme densification of current metropolitan areas, and a renewed focus on the preservation of the countryside beyond their limits.

China: Three Case Studies

Based in Shanghai, Mars has spent several years investigating the physical implications of rapid urbanization. China is home to four of the largest cities in the world - Shanghai, Beijing, Chongqing and Guangzhou - making the country an apt case study. While breakneck urbanization from the 1990s and the first decade of this century prompted the Chinese government to roll-out solutions to cities' seemingly unstoppable spread, few of those strategies have proven effective.

China's rapid urbanization went hand-in-hand with tremendous economic growth, making the model seem more than interesting to other emerging economies. In many cases, China's demonstrably problematic pattern of urban development isn't just emulated, it's directly exported. The effect is most visible in sub-Saharan Africa, with major urban development projects in Angola, Nigeria,

Kenya and Ethiopia that are increasingly being financed, designed and built by Chinese firms.

From a western perspective it is easy to relinquish the Chinese planning model as a failure. In many respects this would be shortsighted. Compactness, high-end transit, and affordability are some of the key features that belong in a sustainable planning model for rapidly urbanizing regions. However, according to Mars, a number of the hallmarks of Chinese urbanism are unfit for exportation and flawed. Not only is its fabric coarse and fragmented, for example, new projects split off from existing fabric, and planning relies on blueprints projected onto green fields. He posits that this leads to 'crude and simplistic outcomes, a diminishing of any existing complexity, and the ultimate erosion of surrounding countryside through relocation and exurbanization.'

'Planning,' he explains, 'is intrinsically unable to move away from this simplification of the urban landscape.' Together the shortcomings of China's urban growth support his hypothesis that sustainability can only be achieved through extreme densification.

Beijing: A Scattered City

Take Beijing, China's capital and home to an estimated 21.7 million inhabitants - already perilously close to population cap of 23 million by 2020, announced in China's 13th Five-Year Plan (2016-2020).[2] Much like rings of a tree, the city's growth pattern is clearly evidenced from above: at its historic heart, finely textured *hutongs* - dense networks of alleys housing shared courtyard dwellings - fast give way to big-box architecture along their outer edge: gargantuan, statement structures that lent the city economic credence, all the while supporting claims of China's "architects' playground" moniker of the early twenty-first century.

Moving further out, beyond the fourth of the metropolis' seven ring roads, the urban fabric becomes noticeably less dense. Decidedly pedestrian-unfriendly avenues and roads link oversized blocks, making car ownership a necessity for most who live here. The typography presents a markedly different lifestyle option compared to the centre's once eminently walkable scale. Moving out farther still, one finds manufacturing plants both recent, as well as those forced into the city's extremities due to constraints of cost and size.

In terms of spatial distribution, Beijing is unremarkable. However, its scale tells a different story. Like a gravitational pull, the pushing-out of industry moves facilities and plants closer and closer to the city limits of neighbouring Tianjin, itself a metropolis of more than 15 million - and growing. As a result, the once rural expanse between the two cities is currently what Mars terms a grey zone - an unsustainable hybrid of urban and rural, with the latter being gradually eked away in the name of costs. Increasingly hard to manage or distinguish, the qualities of both urban and rural conditions are lost.

Shanghai: A Split City

Where Beijing has been allowed to expand its limits largely unchecked, the same cannot be said of Shanghai, where a planned expansion has failed to merge with the original centre in terms of complexity, culture, and arguably, attractiveness.

A poster child for China's rapid "opening up," Shanghai's signature skyline has become synonymous with China's economic success. However, said skyline - Lujiazui, and its current highest-rise trinity of Shanghai World Financial Center, Jinmao Tower, and most recent addition, Shanghai Tower - represent a second and unsustainable example of Chinese expansion: a Split City Model.

The district sits in Pudong, an area located on the eastern bank of the Huangpu River that bisects Shanghai. Positioned diametrically opposite the city's historic centre of Puxi, and ear-marked as a financial zone from the outset, building began in 1988 on empty land. Far from a city of two halves, a total lack of organic growth has seen the east side of the river developed as a one-generational city, entirely disparate from its longer-standing, richly complex counterpart.

With a close-knit texture of *lilongs* - interconnected lanes housing residential communities - as well as the architectural legacies of historic foreign occupations, Puxi has developed over centuries to accommodate a diversity of functions. In stark contrast, the financial centre of Lujiazui was largely realized in little under 25 years, with its planned purpose - finance - dictating composition and form. The result is a highly controlled physical environment of impossibly wide avenues and high-rise buildings that quite aside from issues of regulation, are generally out-priced for residential purposes.

With little available space in the already densely packed west side of the city to accommodate Shanghai's steadily growing population, the market has instead looked to Pudong's hinterland, beyond the dizzying towers and expansive boulevards of dedicated finance zone, Lujiazui. Organic growth denied, it is the housing market itself - rather than lifestyle or need - that has dictated the spatiality and form of Shanghai's continued roll-out of new residential buildings.

The extreme density represents an invaluable resource: human capital. But as Pudong shows, once the concept of "compact city" is applied to extremes, fabric disintegrates. In Shanghai, this is witnessed by clearly delineated units, sealed off by infrastructure, invariably taking the form of copy-paste tower blocks. Disconnected from the centre and adjacent neighbourhoods, they mark an erosion of community, and a city divided. Mars' main concern: Unlike Puxi across the river, Pudong represents an inelastic urban system, which is virtually impossible to improve on a structural level.

The Satellite City

It is a third trajectory that is arguably the greatest cause for concern, as it is precisely this model that is currently being exported globally. Satellite cities, rolled out at high speed as a planning tool to alleviate urban sprawl in existing metropolises compound China's already expansive grey areas by creating supersized urban clusters with little in the way of spatial cohesion between.

Some become so-called "ghost cities." Worse, others prove successful, setting off their own instances of fragmented urban expansion.

The satellite city is by default inward-looking. As an insular model, it allows planners to avoid the context - as opposed to engaging granular fragments of grey zones that surround any project. A high demand for mass housing and rapid rates of urbanization make fast-growing economies common candidates for the Satellite solution. As Mars notes, 'Urgency gives planners an excuse to produce projects that are alien to their environment.'

In China, the failings of these three trajectories - Scattered City, Split City and Satellite - are visible in the steadily expanding grey zones between established urban centres. This is a direct result of cities expanding beyond their borders, and the subsequent pull between urban overspills. Oftentimes, the effect is compounded by informal manufacturing or the relocation of industry away from housing areas.

Highlighting the ultimate spatial diffusion of urban and rural programmes and economies is the 160 kilometre train journey between Shanghai and neighbouring Hangzhou. The distance now reveals an almost entirely hybridized landscape, not only in terms of spatiality, but also of ecology and socioeconomics.

A Dual Approach to Managing Urbanization

The physical implications of urbanization may be most visible in China, and increasingly in rapidly developing markets - but that is not to say that traditionally established economies, like, for example, the Netherlands are immune from their cities spreading in a way that eats into rural areas, and compromises quality of living for all. Simply put, creating sustainable solutions for unstoppable urbanization is nothing if not a global issue.

On a practical level, cities cannot be simply sealed off. 'To give a city physical limits is a falsehood,' Mars concedes: Rural to urban migration will continue, and cities as dynamic entities, will respond. However, rather than be allowed to expand territories exponentially, planners must instead find ways to densify existing centres, creating compact urban cores capable of absorbing urbanization, 'Like a black hole.' These centres, Mars says, should intensify urban gravitational pull, and as such, naturally diminish rural dispersion and fragmentation of the city's edge.

For Mars, innovative approaches to mapping both urban and rural areas, as well alternative data sets, reveal a two-pronged, outside-in solution. In order to intelligently plot where densities should be located, he proposes tracing existing road and public transport networks to ensure an optimal one-hour commute radius from the city centre, thereby ensuring residents' access to amenities and jobs. The same approach can be extended to parks and green spaces; as well as pre-existing energy lines, particularly renewable. In other words: focusing on what is already in place - before considering building anything new.

Overlaying these alternative data sets identifies areas for refinement, where a pre-existing urban fabric could become more closely knit, more dense, in a way that augments quality of life for residents. In doing so, planners shape pockets of accessibility that are conducive to community - as opposed to endless outlying peripheries and grey zones. By moving first from suburbs to the centre, such an approach can achieve incremental densification over time.

In addition to the densification of existing centres and suburbs, rural areas also call for our careful consideration. ‘Only by putting as much emphasis on the other side of the border do you begin to achieve what is otherwise impossible,’ notes Mars, citing access to technology as fundamental in this regard. Focussing attention away from smart cities, and instead to smart *countryside*, may help mitigate some of the fundamental drivers for urbanization, particularly education and employment, and by extension, poverty. ‘A non-urbanization urbanization model calls for a mapping of the countryside to propose strategies of e-commerce, e-education, and to add facilities at a local level, without expanding,’ he explains.

Conclusion

Left to expand at their current rate, cities in China and beyond will cause increasingly irreversible environmental damage. Simply put, contemporary models are not tenable. However, it will not be in metropolises themselves that the implications of rapid urbanization will be most acutely felt, but in grey zones: those nebulous areas between urban and rural that are first to succumb to cities’ physical expansion. Vulnerable to poor regulation, grey zones should not be planned upon, argues Mars. Instead, he calls for a greater focus on densifying existing urban centres in order to maintain and promote diversity; as well as an upgrading of technology in rural areas to negate certain of the catalysts behind urbanization.

For planners, China’s cities are not only a valuable case study. Increasingly, they are a very literal blueprint, with

Chinese urbanism being exported to rapidly urbanizing regions globally. But as the exponential growth of China's own cities continues, their historic planning flaws are becoming increasingly evident. To avoid their proven pitfalls being repeated elsewhere, and halt the insidious proliferation of damaging grey zones, planners must fast develop solutions for sustainable growth.

If extreme densification is the only way forward, then we need to carefully study developments in Hong Kong: one of the most densely populated places on the planet. Large-scale developments could lead to severe segregation, argues architect Inge Goudsmit.

Inge Goudsmit/ OMA

Boring Hong Kong

A vertiginous landscape of dazzling towers, connected by a network of escalators and elevated walkways, flanked by verdant green hills, Hong Kong is undeniably breathtaking. Since its ascent to financial powerhouse at the end of the twentieth century, the city's successes have been cemented in unwavering imagery that has become synonymous with Hong Kong: towering skyscrapers, rising from expansive Victoria Harbour, projecting lasers and lights far around the night sky. However, as Inge Goudsmit, Associate at OMA Hong Kong explains, these popular signifiers tell only half the story.

A remarkable city shaped by a unique history, Hong Kong's trajectory from a cluster of fishing villages to the world's fourth-most densely populated territory makes it a case study worthy of contemporary planners' attention, particularly with regard to its necessary density. Now a Special Administrative Region of the People's Republic of China, the territory has been a stage to a truly unique set of circumstances these past 200 or so years: from its ceding to the British Empire in 1841, to a place of political asylum for Mainland Chinese fleeing Mao Zedong's oppressive regime during the 1940s and 1950, to today's "one country, two systems" formula.

These chapters have seen Hong Kong's number of inhabitants swell, from a modest 600,000 in 1945 to today's

7.2 million-strong population. The territory has responded admirably in managing this influx. For example, thanks to a prevailing typography of tall residential towers, its density currently counts 6,700 people per square kilometre territory-wide, with peaks of 111,000 in certain urban areas.[1] Throughout its 1,100 square kilometre region, Hong Kong's highly efficient and partially privatized MTR, or Mass Transit Railway, keeps masses moving with impressive efficiency. Meanwhile, the company's commercial arm has shaped the city's transport-oriented development, or TOD. From multiple vantage points, the metropolis' impressive infrastructure makes Hong Kong a model, a true "future city."

The superlative nature of the city's successes extends to its flourishing economy. Currently Asia's most significant financial centre, recent years have seen Hong Kong emerge as true billionaire's playground: according to a Wealth-X Billionaire Census they numbered 93 in 2018 - placing it second only to New York.[2]

But as Goudsmit explains, to look beyond Hong Kong's gleaming skyscrapers, uncompromising efficiency and unmistakable financial clout reveals a very different side to this most complex of cities. The territory's necessary density, driven by ongoing urbanization as well as a challenging topography, has created a city of extremes that serves as a clear indicator of an insurmountable wealth gap.

This density is typified at one end by high-end and middle class private housing compounds, oftentimes integrated with commercial ventures and propelling Hong Kong's lucrative real estate market. At the other are public housing developments, often located in "New Towns":

satellite cities comprising public and private estates, and created first and foremost to solve Hong Kong's housing shortage. The scale of the individual estates is massive, forming islands within the New Towns, further inflated as most private compounds are gated. Notable exceptions aside, many present enclaves of poverty throughout the territory. At risk of segregation, they become obstacles to social cohesion and integration.

In contrast to their stark demographical differences, the massive scale of both private and public development models results in a pervasive typological and aesthetic homogeneity. Referencing French theorist and philosopher Guy Debord's Situationist Movement, particularly the group's criticism of the fragmentization of society due to capitalism, Goudsmit argues that Hong Kong emerges as a "boring city."[3]

By examining the city's current and historical approach to public housing developments, as well as private models, Goudsmit reveals a parallel Hong Kong. Outside of central areas, its density becomes not a triumphant achievement, but a barrier to social emancipation that once in place, becomes difficult to rectify. Viewed through this lens, Hong Kong's concrete forest of cookie-cutter towers in housing estates can be read as monuments to ongoing social inequality, fuelled by complex political and economic forces. 'Many factors of society play a role in the shaping of its housing sector,' she observes. 'They create long-lasting impact.' With extreme densification emerging as the most viable solution to meet the challenges of global urbanization, what lessons - both positive and negative - can be learned from Hong Kong?

Hong Kong: A History of Density

Buoyed by political and economic refugees and migrants from Mainland China, Hong Kong's population swelled in the middle of the twentieth century. Many settled in subdivided units of tenement buildings, or else informal huts on accessible land at the fringes of the city. Squalid and overcrowded, conditions continued to deteriorate as more and more incomers - almost all of whom were men - crossed the border. Overcrowding quickly became an issue, with accommodation at such a premium that residents would sleep in shifts, according to whatever work they could find. In this way multiple people per bed was commonplace.

On Christmas Day, 1953, a fire ripped through the Shek Kip Mei squatter settlement, leaving some 53,000 people homeless. The scale of the catastrophe forced the colonial government to finally and decisively turn its attention to Hong Kong's growing housing and migrant crises. Within two months, the then governor, Alexander Grantham, launched the city's first public housing development: the Shek Kip Mei Housing Estate. Resistant to fire and floods, and connected to the city's water and sanitation services, homes marked a significant upgrade on the rudimentary shacks that stood before. Nonetheless, conditions were cramped: 29 seven-storey blocks, each accommodating some 2,500 residents across individual units measuring just 2.4 by 4 metres, and designed for five people. With their galleries, or "elevated streets," these housing blocks were designed after the model of the tenement houses. As such, they allowed for social life and small-scale manufacturing businesses, hence representing a successful evolution of the mixed city model.

By 1961, the population had grown to over three million people, almost half of whom were under the age of 25. Spurred on by events unfolding north of the border in Mainland China, pro-communist sympathizers led protests against the British Hong Kong government, culminating in a wave of riots in 1967.

With order restored, by the early 1970s the city's initial wave of migrants started to assume ownership of their new home: no longer newcomers, or even first generation in some cases, many had brought family and loved ones to join them in Hong Kong. With a population now numbering almost four million people, all expected rights, recognition, and above all, provision of adequate housing.

With overcrowding at critical levels, the Hong Kong government looked increasingly to the British model of garden cities - or "New Towns," as they came to be known - as a solution to the mounting housing crisis. The first of these self-contained communities was Wah Fu Estate, largely completed by 1971 and aimed towards more affluent public residents rather than the lowest income groups. Located away from urban areas, in addition to 18 residential blocks, the development featured several primary and secondary schools, shops, and public transportation facilities.

With moderate density, Wah Fu was a starting point for future evolutions of the New Town model. Moving forward, however, the typology's exponential increase in densification served to deter the moneyed middle classes, and instead drew almost exclusively lower income groups - new migrants in particular.

Nonetheless, and buoyed by the initial promise of the New Town paradigm, the government forged ahead, and in 1972, announced its Ten-Year Housing Programme. Aimed at providing quality housing for 1.8 million people over a decade, it saw the formation of both the Hong Kong Housing Authority and multiple New Towns throughout the territory.

Home to Haves and Have Nots

At the other end of the spectrum is Mei Foo Sun Chuen. Built around the same time, it was Hong Kong's first large-scale private estate, and built to respond to the demands of a growing middle class with money to spare. With an active public plinth boasting shops, a wet market, and parking areas, the compound emulated the street, albeit in a much denser form. Once home to some 70,000 residents, it is still one of Hong Kong's largest housing developments.

Despite their differing demographics, both Mei Foo Sun Chuen (private) and Wah Fu (public) can be categorized as "island developments." Each built by a single developer and housing over 3,000 people or 1,000 households, today, they accommodate over 60 per cent of the total population of Hong Kong.

By the beginning of the 1980s, Hong Kong's move from a manufacturing to service economy - finance in particular - had taken hold. As people became richer, they looked to alternative ways to invest their money, with real estate emerging as particularly lucrative. Right before, in 1979, the MTR was opened: in every sense, Hong Kong's population - now five million and growing - was going places.

Around this time, and at opposite ends of the city, two very different housing developments were taking shape that would come to define Hong Kong's polarities, and highlight the insurmountable gulf between the territory's haves and have nots.

First was Tai Koo Shing, representing a new typology for a major private housing estate and completed in the early 1980s. Located in Quarry Bay in the east of Hong Kong Island, its 61 residential towers offered a range of apartment types, sizes and configurations. Most striking was its mix of programming: the city's first podium tower with a shopping mall underneath, it created an altogether different kind of public space for residents in Hong Kong. 'It was aimed at a higher segment of the market,' Goudsmit explains. 'Residents would wander through the developer-managed mall, past its shops, for a public space that also brought a lot of commercial benefit to the developers themselves.' Fast forward to today, and the model of mall-plus-residential tower has become a familiar paradigm for Hong Kong.

Concurrently in the north-western New Territories, the public housing blocks of Hong Kong's largest New Town to date were rising from a vast area of reclaimed land. Called Tin Shui Wai, its remote location and low cost accommodation in compact flats resulted in a mainstay of new immigrants from mainland China, many of whom were unemployed and still adjusting to urban life. Tin Shui Wai became a microcosm of Hong Kong's inequality. Now home to some 300,000 people, in the early 2000s the satellite earned the depressing moniker of "city of sadness" due to its disproportionately high rate of suicides and homicides.

'Tin Shui Wai marks the huge disconnect between public and private housing in Hong Kong,' explains Goudsmit. 'One hundred times more dense than the Dutch city of Utrecht, it is completely full, there is simply no space left.'

Land Price

A backdrop to these extremes is Hong Kong's flourishing open market economy. Although a portal for vulnerability - witnessed by the bursting of the property bubble after the 1997 Asian Financial Crisis and Hong Kong Handover, and to a lesser extent, during the SARS epidemic of 2003 - for the most part, the model has served Hong Kong well. Its economy continues to grow, and stands today as the world's 35th largest.

With all land owned and leased out by the state - similar to *Erfpacht* in the Netherlands - land receipts represent the Hong Kong government's most significant revenue source. The land premium collected by the government is channelled into the capital works reserve fund, whose large-scale infrastructure projects continue to draw criticism for scale, cost and grandiosity.

A policy of selling land to the highest bidder - regardless of design - has propelled a handful of real estate tycoons to billionaire status; with just one exception, Hong Kong's wealthiest are all property developers. 'It's real estate tycoons and the government who most benefit from high land prices and low tax, and the subsequent monopolistic rights of developers,' says Goudsmit.

The outcomes of this high price, low tax model are

manifold, and its social repercussions complex. Because it is only accessible to the biggest, richest, and most established developers, the arrangement minimizes competition and forces a high cost threshold. For many, the resulting housing is simply unaffordable, and in 2017, a report by property agency Midland Reality placed the average cost per square metre in Hong Kong at about 16,500 USD, while there are reports of over 50,000 USD per square metre.'[4,5]

These sky-high property prices, and monopoly of only big name developers all feeds in to Hong Kong's dismal Gini coefficient (a measure of income distribution between richest and poorest percentiles). From Oxfam's most recent Hong Kong Inequality Report:

> "...The Gini coefficient based on post-tax post-social transfer monthly household income was 0.473 in 2016, which is worse than other developed economies (e.g Singapore 0.356, United States 0.391, United Kingdom 0.351, Australia 0.337, Canada 0.318, Netherlands 0.266). The median monthly household income of the top decile is 44 times greater than that of the lowest decile in 2016, which it was only 34 times in 2006. The number of poor households has reached up to 530,000, of which 300,000 are working poor households; further, over 1.3 million people live in poverty. In May 2018, the total net worth of the wealthiest 21 mega-tycoons in Hong Kong amounted to HK$1.83 trillion, which is equal to the Hong Kong government's fiscal reserves. Nonetheless, a profits tax at the rate of 16.5% paid by corporations run by these mega-tycoons is still significantly lower than the average tax rates in

the Organisation for Economic Co-operation and Development (OECD) and G20 members..."[6]

A comparison of Hong Kong's economic and housing conditions reveals an environment of monstrous disparity, with residents trapped in a density whose contributing factors - a history of migration, on-going urbanization, widespread poverty, and an insurmountable wealth gap - render any rebalancing all but impossible. Increasing pressure comes nowadays from wealthy Mainland Chinese investing in the city, driving up prices even further. Without significant government intervention, any end to the territory's segregation between rich and poor, private and public, seems remote.

Increasingly, the effect of this imbalance is being felt beyond the confines of housing estates themselves, and is eking out onto street level. The city's once fine-grained network of alleys and bridges is being swallowed up by new residential compounds, taking with it Hong Kong's traditional wet markets, community facilities such as playgrounds, as well as small-scale informal businesses. Public spaces are the first to succumb to Hong Kong's ongoing transformation, and today, only 2 per cent is zoned for public areas - translating to just 2sqm per person, about a third compared to other major Asian cities. 'Hong Kong's housing landscape delivers a segregation that is set in stone,' observes Goudsmit. 'Its long-lasting effects convey a clear message to planners: what we build now is going to stay for a very, very long time.'

Lessons from Hong Kong

Today's global trend towards urbanization shows no signs of abating. In order to manage cities' populations, their physical growth, and the environmental impacts the shift inevitably entails, extreme densification is key. However, as Hong Kong so acutely demonstrates, left unchecked, the approach carries potential for wide-reaching social repercussions.

In spite of its essential - not to mention *impressive* - density, housing in Hong Kong has been allowed to develop in a way that reinforces the physical and social segregation between rich and poor, the haves and the have nots. In terms of public housing, large-scale homogeneous estates, often sited far from downtown Hong Kong, simply cannot cater to a required diversity of needs. Rather, they become a magnet for society's most vulnerable: new immigrants, the unemployed, elderly, and poor.

On the flip side, prevailing land policies have facilitated run-away real estate prices in equally enclosed enclaves, with housing costs that are prohibitive to a vast majority of Hong Kong people. That they are commonly managed by developers themselves further exacerbates their isolation, fuelling fragmentation: 'Private governance of housing estates creates black holes in the state structure, causing the government to retreat,' explains Goudsmit.

For planners and architects seeking to densify existing cities, Hong Kong's breakneck development presents important learnings. Concrete in every sense of the word - that is, both materially and in terms of its functional rigidity - its build environment has proven painfully inflexible. To avoid islands and enclaves of isolation, of richer and of poorer, experimentation with smaller scale housing solutions, integrated into existing urban fabric, is key. 'Once the infrastructure is built, it's hard to radically change,' concludes Goudsmit. 'Nevertheless, there are ways to develop this. From a government level, a top down approach of smaller systems, more focused on design and quality - as opposed to the highest bidder - would make a real difference. Hong Kong should look back to its older mixed use models.'

Research can reveal overlooked and new opportunities for urban development, argues New York-based architect Adam Frampton. Looking beyond existing established big-developer models, he reveals pockets of opportunity for new housing prototypes.

Adam Frampton/ Only If

Irregular Development

'Architecture with a capital A is associated with the exceptional and the different. Housing is concerned with the everyday.' So says architect Adam Frampton, principal of New York City architecture and urban design studio, Only If, a practice he runs together with his partner, Karolina Częczek. While practicing across a range of scales and typologies, Frampton's personal experience of high density cities and the housing crises they face sparked a specific interest in irregular development. His research shows that even the most saturated of cities harbour plots of land that although small in size and non-uniform in shape, are nonetheless available for development. These overlooked areas, he argues, present an ideal participation model for young architecture practices, as well as viable residential solutions for cities struggling to house an ever-inflating populous - including Amsterdam.

The world over, housing represents cities' mainstay. With urbanization continuing apace, this allocation is only set to increase. And yet, affordable housing remains beyond the reach of many. In developed economies, one driving factor is a fundamental change to the housing market itself, highlighted in a recent address by United Nations special rapporteur on adequate housing, Leilani Farha: 'Housing has lost its social function and is seen instead as a vehicle for wealth and asset growth. It has become a financial commodity, robbed of its connection to community, dignity and the idea of home.'[1]

Invariably taking the form of penthouse-topped high-rises and luxury developments, the unchecked growth of this 'vehicle for wealth'-type housing damages cities on several levels. First, it compromises societal diversity, spelling clear repercussions on community. It limits models of both production and finance to repetitive formulas, favouring big-name developers. And at ground level, it further dices and cleaves already complex urban fabrics, leaving in its wake jagged plots deemed worthless by these very same developers. Collectively, however, the potential of these slivers is significant - particularly with regard to housing.

Frampton's international career has taken him to a handful of highly developed cities rightly described as saturated and dense. However, alternative mapping reveals another reality sandwiched between New York's skyscrapers, or Hong Kong's extensive walkways, or even Rotterdam's recent proliferation of ambitious towers. The housing challenges faced by all three calls for a timely reappraisal of these overlooked areas.

Working against a backdrop of political uncertainty and profit-driven market forces, Frampton is representative of a young generation of architects for whom contemporary housing challenges reignite an interest in the low-rise efficiency of Modernism. Having presented his concept for Irregular Development at the Shenzhen and Hong Kong Bi-City Biennale of Urbanism/ Architecture in 2017,[2] and with several US-based projects currently underway, he believes that a remapping of cities, and rethinking of their overlooked spaces, reveals alternative approaches to urban development, including much-needed additional and affordable housing.

Hong Kong: An Alternative Perspective

Prior to his move to New York, Frampton worked as an Associate at OMA in both the Netherlands and Hong Kong, where he lived for almost four years. With an estimated population of around 7.5 million, all crammed into a diminutive territory of just 1,100 sqm, a density of 6,300 people per square kilometre[3] makes the special administrative region the fourth-most condensed urban area on earth.

These conditions have uniquely shaped the city of Hong Kong. On the one hand, they have given rise to its now iconic skyline of gleaming skyscrapers and impressive network of footbridges and walkways. But looking beyond - or rather around, *through*, and even *under* - the metropolises' most visible infrastructure reveals a system yet more complex, in which the binaries of public versus private, inside versus out, and above versus below collapse.

By mapping above- and below-ground walkways, both formal and informal, Frampton and his co-authors present an alternative picture of Hong Kong in the 2012 publication, *Cities Without Ground: A Hong Kong Guidebook*. Highlighting a flip side to the official structures for which the city is better known, the work resolutely counters the assertion that Hong Kong lacks public space. In doing so, the project points to ways in which examining cities abroad can reveal overlooked outcomes of - and by extension, opportunities *for* - urban development.

Leftover Land: Fake Estates and Irregular Development

On relocating to New York in 2013, Frampton once again turned to alternative means of mapping the city in order to better understand his new home. Known for its grid, formulated in the Commissioners' Plan of 1811, at first glance, the metropolis' general layout presents few surprises. 'But what's interesting is that it's not a tabula rasa, there were things that existed prior,' explains Frampton. Historical landownership, surveying accidents, and train and utility easements have all created interruptions in the grid, resulting in irregular parcels of land dotted throughout the city. Overlooked, and atypical in both shape and size, the uncovering of these irregular plots proved the starting point for further research, and new speculative proposals for these scattered sites.

The approach recalls the work of architect-turned-artist, Gordon Matta-Clark, and in particular, Fake Estates, a project concerning empty spaces, land ownership, and value. The work saw Matta-Clark purchase 15 parcels of land from the City of New York in the early 1970s, documenting each through deeds and documentation, photography and video. Until around 1980, the city would routinely auction off narrow, inaccessible, or otherwise impractical slivers of land generated through zoning or surveying anomalies. With any longterm intentions for the land left unknown, after the artist's death in 1978 the plots were eventually reverted to the city due to unpaid taxes.[4]

But almost regardless of objectives - that is, whether the act of purchasing the land was the artwork itself; or whether the artist envisioned micro-projects throughout his scattershot empire - Matta-Clark's project continues to speak to Frampton's present-day purpose. That is, to explore the speculative potential of even the tiniest pockets of land, particularly with regard to function, form and value.

With this in mind, Frampton and Częczek used GIS software to map all vacant irregular lots in New York City. The process revealed a total of 3,600 plots, all of which remain unused. Almost all are a result of zoning codes: for example, regulations prohibit the development of very narrow slices of land, under 5.5 metres in width. The same applies to areas less than 93 sqm in area. But by organizing these vacant lots by size, type and shape, Frampton and his colleagues demonstrated that although unconventional in form, and currently problematic in terms of zoning restrictions, New York's empty land nonetheless presents exciting potential. As a starting point for new hypothetical housing typologies for New York, the research has since become reality, with a string of builds on leftover and residual land around existing developments.

'Much of the activity of the city is big developers working with established architects,' observes Frampton. 'Yet housing is 80 to 90 per cent of the city. This could be an opportunity for young architects to enter the market.'

Housing in Crisis

Certainly, New York is in urgent need of alternative housing typologies. A 2018 Census Bureau's Housing and Vacancy Survey pointed to 247,977 empty apartments in the city, up 35 per cent since 2014, and amounting to more than 11 per cent of the rental market.[5] To an overwhelming extent, these vacancies are a reflection of the city's astronomical property prices, which at the time of a 2018 report by real estate and data analytics firm Neighborhood X was $19,000 per square metre in Manhattan.[6]

At the same time, more than 400,000 New Yorkers currently live across 325 public housing developments in five boroughs. According to data published by New York City Housing Authority, another 209,180 families were on the waiting list as of May 2018.[7]

Painting a bleaker picture still, and reinforcing the need for radical interventions to the city's residential landscape, advocacy organization Coalition for the Homeless describe New York City's homelessness as having 'reached the highest levels since the Great Depression of the 1930s.' Each night in November 2018, more than 60,000 homeless people made use of the city's municipal shelter system.[8]

'It's a crisis of housing that's created and perpetuated by political and economical forces,' notes Frampton. 'Architects can have some role in imagining new realities for cities, and inventing new models.'

Experiments in Irregularity: Narrow House

In 2018, Frampton's research into the speculative potential of New York City's anomalous plots became reality, as construction began on Narrow House. Located in Brooklyn's Bedford Stuyvesant neighbourhood, it occupies a formerly vacant site of just four metres wide and 30 metres in depth. Although typical for cities such as Amsterdam, its small size rendered the area prohibited for development under New York City zoning regulations. However, thanks to a legal loophole - the lot preexists the introduction of its current code - Only If was authorized to begin construction on a low-cost prototype property that Frampton believes presents a feasible model for the infill of other vacant lots in New York, and ultimately, be exported to cities worldwide.

'You're working within this very constrained context, where shape is dictated by the zoning envelope. The internal organization of the building becomes very important,' he explains.

The solution was a split-level arrangement, effectively modelling the house as a staircase. Avoiding the need for corridors, the approach sees each room sit on its own landing.

As construction continues, Only If is looking at ways in which the prototype could be scaled to a block or even city level, incorporating different densities to match metropolises' varied - yet undeniably increasing - housing requirements.

Conclusion

'There's a political role that architects have to play to reach beyond architecture, and engage bigger social and political questions, especially in such a strange political moment,' concludes Frampton. In a climate of unprecedented change, driven by factors spanning everything from urbanization and globalization, to the unfolding role of digitalization, architects must continually look to other types of cities abroad, as well as seek overlooked opportunities at home, to optimize how we live and create new models beyond the exclusive - and increasingly untenable - profit-driven developer/architect prototype. To do so calls for research and mapping to rethink spaces both public and private, with housing emerging as cities' most urgent issue not just in New York, but globally. 'Modernists, through their focus on housing, were always talking about the possibility to construct society. As architects, maybe we forget that.'

Migration is a key contributor to urbanization, and therefore an important topic for architects and planners alike. A tangled and oftentimes deeply emotional issue, the drivers of migration may be manifold and complex. Planners have a role to play in creating urban centres not just capable of absorbing and welcoming outsiders, but optimizing the impact of our increasingly diverse communities.

Miguel Gentil Fernández/ Baum Arquitectura

Planning for Migration

'Tensions are an ultimate feature of the urban fact, either subtle or explicit, solved or unsolved,' states Miguel Gentil Fernández, co-founder and partner at Seville-based architecture office, Baum. Speaking to the increasingly pressing issue of migration, his comment recalls another architect of Seville, Carlos García Vázquez, who in his prophetic 2005 book, *Ciudad Hojaldre*, asserted that, 'Cities are not fully possible without conflict.'[1] Showing no sign of slowing, migration will continue to be an important source of growth for world cities, with migrants playing a massive role in the future metropolis. And yet, it is a topic that is too often overlooked by planners. To avoid becoming cities of insiders and outsiders, our urban centres must become resilient, and be able to adapt to this vibrant society.

Whether it's with just the clothes on their backs or with removal trucks full of possessions, however migrants leave a place, and wherever they go, they take with them their identities, culture and conventions. With global urbanization driving people to cities like never before, planners and architects must not only accommodate growing populations in terms of public facilities and housing, but also build urban environments for increasingly diverse communities. In order to create cities that include not marginalize, soften tensions, and mitigate fear of the unknown both on the part of newcomers as well as natives, planners must expand their remit and thinking.

This means looking beyond the visible manifestations of migration, and seeking ways to engage politically with cities.

Immigration is a defining issue of our times. From images of columns of Syrian migrants crossing Europe by foot in 2015; to controversy surrounding Donald Trump's proposed wall between the US and Mexico; and concerns surrounding increasing numbers of immigrants being cited as a key decider in the UK's landmark Brexit referendum of 2016, the how, why and where of migration has a clear domino effect. Planners have a responsibility to create environments capable of absorbing these social and political repercussions. 'Architecture has an agency in the actions and societies that unfold within the space it is defining. It cannot be neutral, but it rather should become a catalyst towards certain situations and not others. Architecture, and even more clearly, urban planning, has a social and political responsibility in the construction of an integrative society,' argues Gentil Fernández.

First, who are we talking about? With their differentiation serving as key deciders for receiving countries in deciding individuals' legal rights, it is important to define the concepts of "migrant" and "refugee." According to UNHCR:

> 'A "migrant" is fundamentally different from a refugee. Refugees are forced to flee to save their lives or preserve their freedom, but "migrant" describes any person who moves, usually across an international border, to join family members already abroad, to search for a livelihood, to escape a natural disaster, or for a range

of other purposes. However, refugees and migrants often employ the same routes, modes of transport, and networks.'[2]

As UNHCR's definition shows, the drivers behind today's migratory movements are manifold and complex. Furthermore, it seems likely that the demographic will continue to diversify and evolve, with climate change emerging as a potential driver of change in the coming years.

Of "Northtopia" and Maps

The wheres and whys that underpin our desire to travel depend entirely on our respective traditions, conditions, and where our conventions place us. These are not only hard to shake, says Gentil Fernández, but have also become institutionalized, rooted deep in individuals' culture.

Take maps: so engrained are their image that for most of us, the merest deviation from the meridians, political divisions, and boundaries of our inbuilt geographic perspectives raises immediate flags. 'Our idea of the world is yet another convention, filtered by politics, wealth, and power-related considerations,' explains the architect. Illustrating his point, Gentil Fernández cites China, where many schools continue to teach a map based on that of sixteenth century cartographer, Li Zhizao, who quite logically positioned China at its centre. The map differs from that taught in Western classrooms, whose centrality is occupied by Europe and North America. The example points to how our tools of geography transmit ideologies - be they nationalistic, or else categorizing systems of governance, ranking wealth, or just about anything else. 'Our mental map of the world is nothing but another convention, a cultural construct assimilated as an absolute,' posits Gentil Fernández.

Maps' conventions - and the convictions they inspire - stay with us, says Gentil Fernández. Also a playwright, in 2018, he penned a drama titled *OFfence*, exploring precisely this phenomenon. In it, lead character, Wilson, shouts, 'The border will travel with you. Even our brains have two fucking hemispheres!' The line underpins Gentil Fernández's observation that while concepts such as *culture* may migrate in both directions, *east and west*, economic migration tends to be considered in terms of *south to north*. This line of travel can also, therefore, be read as a division or boundary line, with "north" weighted more heavily in terms of wealth, and by extension, the advantages affluence affords: education and healthcare, for example. When these abstract lines overlap onto physical territory, they amplify cultural distance - regardless of kilometres, or miles, or degrees. Case in point: the Strait of Gibraltar, which according to UN data, is one of the areas in the world in which these differences are most steep. 'Two worlds, each artificially-made-different, almost touch each other,' surmises Gentil Fernández.

A Spaniard from southern Spain, albeit one whose upbringing and career have seen him travel and live everywhere from Shanghai to New York, Gentil Fernández concedes that he himself holds certain assumptions about Northern Europe as something essentially "better": 'I know that I am not alone in this somewhat secret longing for the golden north,' he admits. Whether or not these hypothesises hold true, he maintains that for many, the idea of a "Northtopia" prevails: that increased order, or wealth, or stability are invariably positioned "north" - wherever that may be.

Immigration to Spain

While the vast majority of migrants arrive in new territories via regular means, and then, quite simply, stay, it is when it comes to the poorest, most desperate people that the situation becomes a humanitarian emergency. Seville, where Baum's office is based, is on the main route north from the Strait of Gibraltar. A way-point on the journey, it is not somewhere most migrants from Africa are willing to stay. Those that do are usually stuck in time-extended temporary situations, notes Gentil Fernández. Not being at their final destination usually puts migrants and refugees in an unstable position, preventing them from settling down.

According to the International Organization for Migration some 172,301 people crossed the Mediterranean Sea to arrive in Europe in 2017 alone. 3,139 weren't so lucky, and died at sea during the attempt.[3] An ostensibly quiet stretch of water, the Mediterranean is nothing if not deadly dangerous. And yet, people continue to cross to what has become a frontier country of Europe, and of "Northtopia." In the case of the Strait of Gibraltar, a meeting point of two vast bodies of water measuring just 14.4 kilometres in width, the tantalizing proximity of two remote levels of life becomes too close to resist. And yet, along the way, migrants find their "Northtopian" idylls moving further and further away.

Hailing from north African nations such as Libya, as well as sub-Saharan countries including Guinea, Senegal,

Sudan, Cameroon, and elsewhere, migrants' respective "Northtopias" may translate to safety and security, economic emancipation, or improved quality of life. Depending on their departure point, the trip could take years, and amount to significant sums of money. This in itself makes the endeavour vulnerable to mafia operations.

Regardless of the driver and catalyst, a common baseline is desperation. How else to account for the use of quite literally toy boats to attempt this most treacherous of crossings? Or indeed, embarking on such a journey when migrants themselves cannot swim? During the 2016 Libya crisis alone, almost 5,000 lost their lives traversing the Mediterranean Sea, according to UNHCR.[4]

'The situation is certainly complex,' concedes Gentil Fernández. 'Any move towards welcoming policies tends to become a "calling effect," which eventually makes the humanitarian crisis worse. Any blockage attempt is conceptually unethical. Both options are political bombs.'

From Arrival to Ambiguity

In recent years, the fraught nature of migrants' journeys has become increasingly visible. Writers including Eduardo del Campo, for example, have given voice to refugees' struggle for survival.[5] Artists have also responded, with the likes of Mexico's Richard Sierra engaging with migration's political, administrative and ethical incoherencies; and Ai Wei Wei's city-wide exhibition for New York in 2017, titled 'Good Fences Make Good Neighbors.'[6,7] At the same time, migrants' plight has become a mainstay of our mass media the world over. And yet, highly publicized images of migrant boats attempting the perilous Strait of Gibraltar crossing represent just the tip of the iceberg. Likewise, the periodic storming of the bladed and deadly perimeter fences of north African Spanish enclaves, Melilla and Ceuta. Europe's only land borders on the continent, in July 2018 a mass breach by almost 700 migrants from sub-Saharan Africa resulted in unprecedented levels of violence between armed enforcement officers and those seeking entry into Ceuta.[8]

But migrants' land or sea crossings tell only part of their story. Should they make it into Spain, individuals are sorted into those coming from countries with bilateral deportation agreements in place, and those without. Almost all are held in police facilities for up to three days. After, they may be sent to a *Centro de Internamiento de Extranjeros*, or CIE, for a maximum of 60 days. These facilities have become a new architectural typology in themselves, almost like a prison, and definitely far from a reception centre. Both UNHCR and Human Rights Watch have repeatedly reported these facilities for not respecting international agreements.[9]

Depending on individuals' legal status, they may be deported during this period, or else released without legal rights - and an obligation to leave the country. 'In this scenario, people find themselves in limbo, neither legal or illegal. This can extend for years,' explains Gentil Fernández.

Thanks in part to the African continent's close proximity, Spain's policy of certain tolerance with regard to immigration, and perhaps also to the country's reputation for multiculturalism, in 2018 the European nation was one of the main entry points for migrants arriving in Europe from Africa by sea. Once again, it was Spain, Italy, and

Greece that came under the most pressure internationally from this recent spike in arrivals. If this pattern is to continue, a diversity of agencies and industries must work together to maintain and improve Spain's systems of welcoming, habilitating, and above all, *integrating* incomers, no matter their onward journey. International cooperation as well as local development is key, maintains Gentil Fernández, particularly with regard to tackling mafia organizations. These criminal groups perpetuate false promises and assumptions of an idealized "Northtopia" he says; controlling them will go some way to easing pressure on both sides.

Planning for Migration

What role could architecture and planning play in ensuring cities are equipped to respond to tides of migrants of all kinds? Could planners' closer engagement help mitigate the very conditions that cause people to leave a place? Are there interventions we could make to manage relations - and tensions - between natives and newcomers? How could cities maintain their openness and connections to avoid becoming an archipelago of fixed, fenced societies?

Urban planners build the foundations of community and society. They facilitate culture and concentration of capital. But in the twenty-first century, their responsibility must also extend to one of the most pressing issue of our times: migration. Because no matter whether they've crossed city lines, international borders, or continents, migrants will play a huge role in the city of the future. Simply put, *they must not be marginalized.*

To that end, architecture and urban planning's

contribution to the refugee crisis should not be limited to the creation of new obscure typologies for dividing people. Rather, there is an important role for architects and planners in envisioning the manner in which cities should react to this complex social situation. The discipline needs to mutate, and develop new and necessary tools to bring people together.

A Starting Point: SI8DO

In addition to commercial projects, Baum also undertakes conceptual design. The office's Seville address, a "Northtopia" for some and waypoint for others, affords daily encounters with the consequences of immigration, both in terms of its opportunities and injustices. This vantage point was the start for SI8DO, a form of urban furniture specifically designed to support - and highlight - a particular branch of immigrants in the city.

Oftentimes finding themselves in a kind of legal limbo - obligated to leave but unwilling or financially unable to do so - hundreds of immigrants from Africa eke out a living in and around Seville by selling packets of tissues at traffic lights. 'This group is very visible,' explains Gentil Fernández of the immigrant subset. 'When you work with the visible part, you create an idea of the total. So a small intervention can create an impact on the whole.'

Often working 12-hour days, these informal salespeople, most of whom are men from north and central Africa, crisscross lines of stationary cars as they queue at red lights. Over weeks, months and years, regular commuters such as Gentil Fernández frequently spot familiar faces among them.

Observing that most spend their days standing, Baum created SI8DO, a seat of perforated metal for either comfort or storage that can be attached to traffic lights. A solution for injecting humanity and stability into this informal workforce's otherwise precarious existence, the proposal won first prize in the 2013 edition of Unpleasant Design competition, an initiative assessing and rewarding positive means of social integration in public spaces.

The project's name comes from NO8DO, Seville's official motto and a rebus translating roughly to 'She [Seville] has not abandoned me,' attributed to thirteenth century King Alfonso X The Wise. Baum's proposal questions this assertion and posits, *Sí me ha dejado*, or 'she let me down.' In doing so, it challenges the role and responsibilities of cities and planners.

A very minor intervention, and parasitic by design, SI8DO won't solve the injustices, challenges, and implications of immigration. But its existence does ask: *What more could we do?*

All over the world, tourism is growing massively, with cities globally now suffering from over-tourism. Only radical solutions can turn the tide, argues Amsterdam-based tourism expert, Stephen Hodes.

Stephen Hodes/ LAgroup

Over-tourism

Since its gradual emergence at the beginning of the nineteenth century, through to a rapid expansion in the 1960s, international tourism has proven more than resilient. Today, leisure travel abroad maintains its position as a cornerstone and driver of globalization. What's more, the trend shows no sign of abating: the first six months of 2018 saw international tourist arrivals grow 6 per cent on the previous year's record growth.[1]

International tourism can bring clear benefits, particularly with regard to local and global economies. Indeed, according to World Travel & Tourism Council, the sector generated $7.6 trillion for the global GDP in 2014.[2] An important source of employment in all corners of the world, it is indicative of increased global mobility and wealth, and may help cultivate more globally minded individuals. After all: *travel broadens the mind.*

However, for the inhabitants of particular tourism hotspots, the impact of mass tourism may be less positive. As visitor numbers grow, cities must balance the needs of an exponentially expanding tourism industry with those of local residents. Recent years have seen resident-led anti-tourism movements emerge in Venice, Barcelona, and Dubrovnik, to name just a few. How can these destinations continue to reap the benefits brought by tourism, without compromising on liveability?

Over-tourism is a challenge currently facing Amsterdam. According to the national statistics office, CBS, the number of visitors staying overnight in the country in 2017 grew almost 9 per cent on the previous year to 42 million, with 37 per cent of all foreign visitors spending an average of 1.9 nights in Amsterdam.[3]

In the Dutch capital, infrastructure is being put in place to accommodate and absorb this annual influx. However, the growth surrounding tourism continues to outpace formal plans currently in place to alleviate its impact. Case in point: Schiphol Airport, where an annual flight quota is already all but met. With plans to expand existing and predominantly private aviation facility, Lelystad Airport, to commercial operations still under debate, Schiphol has been forced to upgrade: a new pier by December 2020, and a new terminal come 2023.[4,5] On a neighbourhood level, a surfeit of Airbnb properties limits affordable housing stock for locals, with landlords preferring more profitable short-term lets to long-term tenancies.

Quite simply, tourism's current rate of growth is not sustainable.

Recent years have seen the city make half-hearted attempts to mitigate the effects of over-tourism on local culture, and on residents - all the while maintaining Amsterdam's attractiveness as a destination. To date, however, these measures have proven inadequate. What is required, asserts Stephen Hodes, partner at consultancy firm LAgroup, is a new paradigm for tourism, and new levels of cooperation across sectors and industries: 'Radical change requires radical measures.'

What Drives International Tourism?

Driving the growth of global tourism is, of course, the growth of the world's population and its middle class. Geopolitics also play a part: in 26 European states, for example, the common visa policy afforded by the Schengen Agreement makes travel within this region comparatively straightforward. And since China's economic reform in the late-1970s, its citizens have enjoyed increasing levels of freedom to travel, with the country's 1.3 billion-strong population considerably boosting tourist numbers.

The world's ever-swelling number of tourists also directly correlates with developments in transportation and transport infrastructure. Air travel, for example, has become second nature to many, as budget airlines compete to win customers' fares. Combine this with an increase in disposable income, marked in part by an expanding middle class, and never before has air travel been so affordable, nor so accessible. On the ground, too, our connections are becoming easier, faster and cheaper thanks to high-speed rail in places like China, the Channel Tunnel in Europe, and for shorter hops or once we're there, options such as Uber, Lyft and so on.

Recent years have seen technology facilitate international tourism even more, with myriad online platforms for booking everything from travel to accommodation in a mere matter of clicks. Social media also plays a part, with (paid) influencers as well as our personal networks contributing to a collective desire and normalization of frequent travel. As Hodes notes, 'The world is coming into our houses and homes.'

Of course, the biggest driver of them all is the sheer number of travellers - and our increasing appetite for adventure. In 2018, international tourists numbered 1.4 billion.[6] According to United Nations World Tourism Organization, by 2030, that number could swell to 1.8 billion tourists globally, amounting to almost one in five people, with significant growth from the Middle East, Asia, and Africa.[7]

An attractive European capital steeped in 'Old World Charm,' Amsterdam has felt the force of this seemingly unstoppable tide of tourism. Rich in art, architecture, and photogenic to boot, the capital city is intrinsically tied to Dutch identity in the eyes of outsiders. According to the Dutch Bureau for Statistics, a majority - almost 80 per cent - of foreign visitors to the country hail from Europe.[8] Nonetheless, the number of intercontinental tourists is rising steadily, and will continue to do so. 'In terms of population growth, Europe is getting smaller. Take Amsterdam, for example: it's growing comparatively slowly, at a rate of around 1 per cent per year. But in terms of number of tourists, we're getting much larger, very quickly,' outlines Hodes.

Simply put, tourism in Europe is nearing saturation point. Hodes explains: 'All of this is about growth - of the world's population, number of travellers, flights, hotels - everything is growing dramatically. But is growth a choice, or something that you just have to accept?'

Can Amsterdam Absorb its Tourism?

While a majority of Amsterdammers are delighted to show off the place they call home, it is becoming increasingly apparent that the city's current levels of tourism are simply not sustainable. The shortcoming is most keenly evidenced in recent years' flight quotas of Schiphol Airport. The third busiest in Europe in terms of passenger volume, it met its 2020 allowance of 500,000 flights annually two years early, in 2018.[9] Officials have now floated the prospect of increasing to 800,000 by 2020, spelling a growth of 60 per cent in just five years.[10] Environmental implications aside, the move would significantly impact quality of life for residents living in the airport's vicinity.

In the city proper, Amsterdam's compact monocentric spatiality is at once a key attraction for incoming tourists, as well as a major factor in compounding congestion of both vehicles and foot traffic - not to mention frequent run-ins with visitors unused to the city's cycle paths. Given the city's most popular sites are all in close proximity - Dam Square, the Red Light District, and Museumplein, to name a few - Amsterdam makes an ideal weekend getaway or day trip. However, these areas fast become concentrated with tourists - much to the frustration of inconvenienced residents. Of particular resentment is the increasing number of low-budget travellers.

The fact that Amsterdam - and therefore, the Netherlands - is more famous abroad for legal prostitution and soft drugs than it is for Mondriaan, the Concertgebouw Orchestra, and Escher is largely the city's own doing. Years of one-track city promotion has generated the image of a European Las Vegas, a veritable 'Sin City.'

In Italy, for example, a chain of coffee shops with the name 'Cannabis Store Amsterdam' has recently hit the headlines. Supreme Court action aside, the fact remains:

the franchise has opened some hundred stores in under a year.[11] In doing so, it appropriates, exploits, and reduces a single facet of the city's identity that bears only minor relation to the wider whole. Writing in Dutch newspaper, *de Volkskrant*, journalist Jarl van der Ploeg posits that the 'Amsterdam Coffeeshop' thus has the dubious honour of joining the likes of the "Chinese Takeaway Restaurant," "American Diner," "Irish Pub," or similarly ubiquitous "Turkish Kebab" store.[12] As such, the genre is far from constructive in terms of tapping a type of tourist who spends more, and whose intentions are more likely to be cultural than purely hedonistic.

And yet, such tourists swarm to Amsterdam in their droves. As a result, the city's highest valued location - the historic canal district - contains the lowest-value activities: coffeeshops, brothels, and Nutella stores. On a nightly basis, stag parties are fuelled by precisely this explosive cocktail of legal marijuana, prostitution, and cheap eateries to stave off the munchies.

Tackling Over-Tourism

None of these issues are new. They are, however, coming to a head, and importantly, to the attention of Amsterdam City Government, which has implemented a number of strategies aimed at making tourism more sustainable. To date, none have been so visible as the drastic steps taken by, say, Boracay in the Philippines, which shut its doors to tourists in 2018 due to the resort's infrastructure not keeping pace with runaway growth. And in Italy, the City of Venice last year launched its #EnjoyRespectVenezia campaign, designed to raise awareness of the impact of tourism, and cultivate responsible, respectful behaviour among visitors. Moreover, the city took the decision to ban large cruise ships in the city centre.[13]

According to Hodes, these same concerns are now palpable in Amsterdam. 'There is a huge groundswell of anti-tourism sentiment in this city, and the government does not want to listen,' he observes. 'At some point, there will be a clash.'

So what steps has Amsterdam taken to manage over-tourism - and why are they proving ineffective? Efforts range from the highly targeted - the 2018 launch of the "Enjoy & Respect" campaign, aimed primarily at stopping offensive behaviour by Dutch and British people aged 18 to 34; to the superficial: the removal of the "I Amsterdam" logo from outside Rijksmuseum in December 2018 after the locale was identified as a 'selfie hotspot.'[14,15]

Other measures, although well-reasoned, prove virtually impossible to police. Take the aim to preserve both local culture, as well as the provision of essential amenities for residents, by the city's government in imposing limits on the number of shops geared directly towards tourists in central Amsterdam. While some are easy to spot - bike rental and ticket outlets, for example - others are less so. In 2018, a cheese shop in the city was closed by the authorities because it was considered to target tourists over local consumers, due to its use of English language in its marketing and stores.[16]

Accommodation for incoming tourists has proven a similarly slippery subject. While measures such as a proposed nightly tourist tax of up to 10 euros (on top of an existing 5 per cent on accommodation) may help deter budget - and by extension, low-spending - visitors, anecdotally, a 2017 "hotel stop" prohibiting the development of new properties is only sporadically enforced. A particular failing of the block is that Amsterdam's 20,000 or so homes and rooms listed with online hospitality giant, Airbnb, are classified not as hotel accommodation, but housing. An attractive option for visitors as well as homeowners, Hodes notes that, 'Amsterdam is the only city in the world where the average Airbnb prices are higher than those of the average hotel prices.'

At the same time, marketing campaigns aimed at drawing tourists' attention to destinations beyond the capital are falling short. 'There's an attempt to take people to other cities, such as Rotterdam, The Hague, and Utrecht,' observes Hodes. However, given the country's current tourism mainstay of short-haul travellers and day-trippers, combined with Amsterdam's strong Dutch identity, a majority of visitors nonetheless choose to pass through the capital. 'These other cities are all great, but don't have the same social or conversational currency as Amsterdam.'

The highest-profile of these measures is a proposed relocation of the cruise terminal to the harbour area, or even further away from the city. The new terminal is aimed at relieving pressure on the city centre. However, cruise ship passengers are arguably the least economically interesting tourist type to visit the city, oftentimes buying little more than a coffee ashore, while eating and sleeping onboard. Although the recent extension of Amsterdam's tourist tax to include cruise passengers will go some way to bridging this economic shortfall, it will likely do little to alleviate shuffling hordes of “locust tourists” bussing in and out of the city for little more than a day trip.

Balancing Tourism

‘We have an obsession with growth,’ says Hodes of our snowballing tourism industry. But while an “always more” approach may reap short-term economic benefits, its longer terms implications are potentially catastrophic.

For example, anti-tourism sentiment is increasingly palpable in cities such as Venice and Barcelona. And elsewhere, a pervasive “dumbing down” of authentic local culture in favour of more tourist-friendly portrayals is becoming depressingly commonplace. ‘Either you turn the city into a Disneyland, or you do something about it. The point is, you have to be radical, there are no half measures,’ warns Hodes. But while managing tourism in a way that caters to all stakeholders - that is, balancing industry needs with those of residents, all the while benefiting from the revenue tourists bring - is far from straightforward, it is essential for sustainability. For Amsterdam, his proposals include a complete hotel stop, followed by a quota system in line with population growth; and access only to cruise ships that are economically interesting and environmentally responsible. ‘Our obsession with growth will kill us, because we think that success means getting bigger, getting more. But if you have fewer people who spend more, you’re economically better off,’ Hodes asserts.

While there can be no one-size-fits-all solution, the current cultural phenomena of over-tourism calls for industries and sectors to work together, and collectively, urgently ask themselves: “What kind of city do we want to live in?" Inevitably, that will call for pressure to be put on the chain across multiple industries and ultimately, closer regulation, be that in the form of caps, quotas, or in some cases, outright blocks.

The world over, attractive tourist destinations such as Amsterdam share one quality in common: they strike a balance between liveability, and physical and cultural accessibility to outsiders. But our consumerist-driven growth obsession jeopardizes this status quo, fuelling resentment of tourists among locals, contributing to climate change, and diluting cities' unique cultural elements. Turning the tide of over-tourism requires our collective action and responsibility - but in the case of Amsterdam, may also offer a unique opportunity to reassert and reframe the city's global reputation.

'We used to be a model city,' describes Hodes. 'We were the first to legalize drugs, first to legalize same-sex marriages, and prostitution - in all these things we took a really unpopular stance and said, "This is what we believe in." We could do this with tourism and become world leaders in solving this problem. But it can't be solely down to government, you have to have industries and institutions on board too.'

Nightlife is a critical part of a vivid and inclusive city with a strong cultural infrastructure. Using the cover of the night, nightclubs could allow for experimentation with new forms and expressions of collectivity, functioning as a parallel universe to the immateriality of the digital age, says David Mulder van der Vegt of XML.

David Mulder van der Vegt/ XML

Bright Lights, Big City

A spiritual home of electronic dance music, Amsterdam and the Randstad are host to a growing number of music festivals, large-scale parties, and mega-clubs. These venues and events have increasingly contributed to Amsterdam as a magnet for runaway tourism. Yet the steady expansion of these commercial festivals comes at the cost of the culture of club life of decades past, argues architect David Mulder van der Vegt, a founding partner of international architecture, urbanism and research agency, XML.

As cities become increasingly global, so too does their nightlife. This is driven first and foremost by digital marketing and social media, with hyper-connectivity leading to an increased homogeneity of music and clubs, their sponsors, DJs and crowds. As such, nightlife today contrasts starkly with the experimentation, locality, and spontaneity associated with, for example, post-war Italy's discos, the most renowned of which were designed by proponents of the Radical Architecture movement. Recalling this most innovative of eras, Mulder van der Vegt asks: what role can architects and planners play in shaping alternative modes of nightlife in ways that encourage collectivity and forge cultural identity?

In terms of Amsterdam's built environment, recent years have seen particular growth. The various plans for the city represent just one of the ways in which Amsterdam is bolstering itself for progress and urbanization. An important driver of incomers to Amsterdam and one of its most distinguishing advantages is culture. This extends to landmark national museums, a flourishing creative industry - and vibrant nightlife.

While city planners have recognized the white cube of the art museum as a crucial programme for the development of attractive cities, the black box of the nightclub is mostly neglected. However, argues Mulder van der Vegt, in successful cities these programmes go together. An interesting night culture draws precisely the creative and entrepreneurial talents that forge cities' global reputations. But more importantly, nightlife is an essential component of a vibrant and inclusive city with a strong cultural ecosystem. Testament to the symbiotic relationship between nightlife, creativity, and growth is Berlin, which has become a magnet for precisely this demographic since the mid 1990s.

Amsterdam's Changing Nightlife

In recent years, Amsterdam's nightlife has undergone significant shifts, with the global festival trend emerging as a powerful shaping force. While clubs have closed, or else been relocated to the city's fringes, the number of festivals taking place in the Netherlands has risen. During the first half of 2017, for example, their numbers rose by 25 per cent on the same period of the preceding year, taking the total number to 145, according to Dance Festival Monitor.[1] And although the same research reported a drop in ticket revenue, 2012 research by Dutch consultancy EVAR Advisory Services pitched the financial flows associated with large-scale (that is, attendance of more than 3,000 people) electronic dance music festivals and events in the Netherlands at €137.4 million - up 67.8 per cent from 2002.[2]

This growth is backdropped by digitalization. From how events and venues are promoted, to the means partygoers use to connect and convene, the internet's impact on everything from sponsorship and tickets sales, to communicating the elusive "soft power" these large-scale festival events afford, is significant. In contrast to clubs in which one was never sure what to expect or whom to meet, social media allows party planners to target specific audiences and organize massive crowds.

At the same time, the globalization and mobility our increasingly connected world affords enables the networking of parties, which risks monopolization of this lucrative market. The very same handful of drinks sponsors or music labels, for example, may organize identikit festivals and events everywhere from New York to Bangkok, Amsterdam to Adelaide. In short, the potential for nightlife's homogenization seems increasingly real. 'The space is getting taken over by commerce, so you get similar rituals of collectivity all over world, all within very similar non-designed eventhall types of physical environment,' says Mulder van der Vegt. 'As architects I think one of the main challenges we have to engage with is what is the meaning of physical space within digital times.'

Architects' Nighttime Potential

Already pivotal in shaping our cities and society, it seems logical that the profession should expand its remit and scope to play a more active role in creating the spaces in which nightlife happens, and bring to them the same standards of inclusivity, diversity, and flexibility applied to other dimensions of city living. In post-war Italy of the 1960s and 1970s, pioneers of the Radical Architecture movement such as Superstudio and Gruppo 9999 did precisely this through nighttime hubs of creativity that attracted, inspired, and engaged luminaries from the realms of fashion, art, architecture and beyond. 'These young, radical, utopian architects used discos as places of experimentation, environments in which to loosen the rules and try things out,' explains Mulder van der Vegt.

Pioneering the genre was Piper in Rome, designed by Manilo Cavalli, Francesco Capolei and Giancarlo Capolei. On opening its doors in 1965, it became a showcase and stage for the most cutting-edge visual art, audio-visual experimentation, and of course, music. The iconic venue inspired yet more eclectic discos across Italy, including Space Electronic in Florence by Gruppo 9999, which used temporary, theatrical installations - including at one point, a vegetable garden - to create alternative environments 'where everything and anything was possible,' describes Mulder van der Vegt. 'These radical discos were also important meeting places for exchanging ideas, escaping the everyday, and losing oneself in a different world, created through design.'

It wasn't only in Italy that creative visionaries were exploring the tensions and possibilities between architecture and art, and in doing so, shaping environments of experimentation, inclusivity, and exchange. In New York, for example, Andy Warhol's Factory was a hangout for liberally minded individuals and as such, a hotbed of multidisciplinary creativity. Echoing the theatrical installations of radical discos, which often incorporated miscellaneous and unexpected materials, the artist's original studio was dubbed "The Silver Factory" due to photographer and filmmaker Billy Name's enveloping of its interior in shards of mirror and tin foil.[3]

A Radical Revival?

As opposed to the decadence and exclusivity of the clubs at the end of the 1980s, a counter-movement arose in unplanned industrial spaces, argues Mulder van der Vegt. A counterculture of hardcore and rave emerged in non-designed venues that gradually became mainstream. This, in combination with the rise of the web, which facilitated the quick mobilization of large groups of people, eventually led to an enormous increase in scale and to the rise of festivals and other large-scale events. 'The club as an undeviating meeting place and place of collectivity lost more and more significance.'

Architects and planners well understand the importance of facilitating societal mix in housing developments and shopping precincts. By revisiting certain of the principles of radical discos, could they bring the same diversity to nightlife? That is the goal of an ongoing project by XML in central Amsterdam, commissioned by the owner of the city's late, great, and notorious RoXY nightclub. The legendary RoXY burnt down in 1999, when sparks from indoor fireworks lit to commemorate the funeral of co-founder, Peter Giele, entered the venue's air circulation systems. The new club is designed by XML with mixed programming in mind. 'It could also be used for art exhibitions during the day,' Mulder van der Vegt suggests. 'Or a co-working space, or temporary studios for students creating large theatrical installations for the evening, so it becomes a kind of night theatre. Our client likes to talk about it as a culture clubhouse, a safe haven for a creative community that should feel at home there.' By creating an architecture that can accommodate diversity in all its manifestations, the building will be an important node in Amsterdam's infrastructure for new ideas and creativity.

Space for Experimentation

In addition to making cities attractive to a particular demographic of incomers, great nightlife lends urban centres a strong cultural backbone that feeds into other areas of society: 'The cover of the night provides a space for experimentation, and from that night, new artists and new movements might arise,' notes Mulder van der Vegt. As prime leisure destinations for a spectrum of people and classes, nightclubs represent a vanguard of this shift. 'By thinking of even small spaces as complete environments that can be changed completely, architecture can help ritualize notions of coming together. A nightclub is a fascinating space in which to explore and experiment with that,' he concludes.

Notes

What Kind of City Do We Want to Be?

1 http://mori-m-foundation.or.jp/english/ius2/gpci2/index.shtml

Bijlmer Blues

1 https://www.facebook.com/50jaarBijlmer/

Participation Matters

1 Jane Jacobs, The Death and Life of Great American Cities (New York: Random House, 1961)

Digital Flexibility

1 https://www.dezeen.com/2018/05/03/frank-gehry-berlin-skyscraper-hines-hochhaus-on-hold/
2 https://www2.holzmarkt.com/
3 https://content.knightfrank.com/research/1026/documents/en/global-residential-cities-index-q4-2017-5413.pdf
4 http://www.stadtentwicklung.berlin.de/wohnen/mietspiegel/index.shtml

The Future of Work

1 https://www.amsterdam.nl/projecten/haven-stad/
2 https://www.geek.com/gadgets/google-uses-high-tech-nap-pods-to-keep-employees-energized-1264430/

Flexible Systems

1 https://www.un.org/development/desa/en/news/population/2018-revision-of-world-urbanization-prospects.html
2 http://worldpopulationreview.com/world-cities/istanbul-population/
3 http://www.hurriyetdailynews.com/istanbuls-share-in-total-gdp-stood-at-31-percent-in-2017-140330
4 https://www.tomtom.com/en_gb/trafficindex/city/istanbul
5 http://www.hurriyetdailynews.com/traffic-is-istanbuls-biggest-problem-istanbul-mayoral-candidate-yildirim-says-140338
6 https://www.theguardian.com/world/2013/may/31/istanbul-protesters-violent-clashes-police
7 https://www.brookings.edu/blog/order-from-chaos/2018/06/19/syrian-refugees-in-turkey-beyond-the-numbers/
8 http://www.urbantactics.org/
9 https://bernardvanleer.org/solutions/urban95/

Smart Cities

1 https://www.theguardian.com/cities/2014/dec/17/truth-smart-city-destroy-democracy-urban-thinkers-buzzphrase

2 http://www.mohurd.gov.cn/jsbfld/201301/t20130131_221676.html

The Grey Zone

1 https://www.un.org/development/desa/en/news/population/2018-revision-of-world-urbanization-prospects.html
2 http://english.gov.cn/policies/latest_releases/2017/09/27/content_281475888642154.htm

Boring Hong Kong

1 https://www.thatsmags.com/china/post/8286/visualizing-urban-density-hong-kong-vs-shanghai-vs-the-world
2 https://www.wealthx.com/report/the-wealth-x-billionaire-census-2018/
3 Guy Debord, La Société du Spectacle, (Buchet-Chastel, 1967, in French; Black & Red, 1970, in English), 166 + 171: "The free space of commodities is constantly being altered and redesigned in order to become ever more identical to itself, to get as close as possible to motionless monotony... While all the technical forces of capitalism contribute toward various forms of separation, urbanism provides the material foundation for those forces and prepares the ground for their deployment. It is the very technology of separation."
4 https://www.reuters.com/article/us-hongkong-economy-property/hong-kong-home-prices-post-record-breaking-growth-in-2017-idUSKBN1FK0E3
5 https://www.scmp.com/property/hong-kong-china/article/2138095/one-four-hongkongers-cant-ever-afford-home-micro-flat-sells
6 https://www.oxfam.org.hk/en/f/news_and_publication/16372/Oxfam_inequality%20report_Eng_FINAL.pdf

Irregular Development

1 https://www.ohchr.org/EN/NewsEvents/Pages/DisplayNews.aspx?NewsID=21253&LangID=E
2 http://szhkbiennale.org/En/Exhibits/details.aspx?id=10000945
3 https://en.wikipedia.org/wiki/Demographics_of_Hong_Kong
4 http://socks-studio.com/2014/10/22/gordon-matta-clarks-reality-properties-fake-estates-1973/
5 https://www1.nyc.gov/assets/hpd/downloads/pdf/about/2017-hvs-initial-findings.pdf; https://www.6sqft.com/nearly-250000-nyc-rental-apartments-sit-vacant/
6 http://www.neighborhoodx.com/blog-national-comparing-prices-across-major-US-cities-august-2017
7 https://www1.nyc.gov/assets/nycha/downloads/pdf/NYCHA-Fact-Sheet_2018_Final.pdf
8 http://www.coalitionforthehomeless.org/wp-content/uploads/2019/02/NYCHomelessnessFactSheet_12-2018_citations.pdf

Planning for Migration

1 Carlos Garcia Vazquez, Ciudad Hojaldre (Barcelona: Editorial Gustavo Gili, 2005)
2 https://emergency.unhcr.org/entry/250459/migrant-definition
3 https://www.telegraph.co.uk/news/2018/09/03/migrant-death-rate-mediterranean-rises-despite-fewer-crossings/
4 https://www.unhcr.org/5aa78775c.pdf
5 Eduardo del Campo, Odiseas (Seville: Fundación José Manuel Lara, 2007)
6 https://ricardosierra.carbonmade.com/
7 https://www.publicartfund.org/ai_weiwei_good_fences_make_good_neighbors/about

8 https://elpais.com/elpais/2018/07/26/inenglish/1532599360_950584.html
9 https://www.hrw.org/news/2017/07/31/spain-migrants-held-poor-condi tions

Over-tourism

1 http://www2.unwto.org/press-release/2018-10-09/international-tour ism-maintains-strong-momentum
2 https://sp.wttc.org/about/media-centre/uniting-travel-statements/2015/ gtac-gs-annoucement/
3 https://www.cbs.nl/en-gb/news/2018/14/tourism-sees-fastest-growth-in-over-ten-years
4 https://www.dutchnews.nl/news/2019/02/schiphol-airport-must-be-able-to-grow-infrastructure-minister-says/
5 https://www.schiphol.nl/en/projects/page/project-new-pier-and-termi nal/
6 https://www2.unwto.org/press-release/2019-01-21/international-tour ist-arrivals-reach-14-billion-two-years-ahead-forecasts
7 https://news.un.org/en/story/2017/12/640512-world-could-see-18-billion-tourists-2030-un-agency
8 https://www.cbs.nl/en-gb/news/2018/14/tourism-sees-fastest-growth-in-over-ten-years
9 https://www.dutchnews.nl/news/2018/02/schiphol-airport-renews-calls-for-increased-flight-movement-cap/
10 https://www.dutchnews.nl/news/2017/07/schiphol-needs-second-termi nal-to-stay-in-airport-big-league/
11 https://www.ildolomiti.it/cronaca/2019/salvini-contro-la-canna bis-light-ma-uno-studio-rivela-i-benefici-per-la-lotta-alla-criminali ta-il-punto-vendita-di-trento-rispettiamo-la-legge-ma-siamo-molto-pre occupati
12 https://www.volkskrant.nl/nieuws-achtergrond/in-italiaanse-winkel straten-walmt-de-cannabis-light-je-tegemoet~b2e8adbe/
13 https://www.bbc.com/news/world-europe-49276730
14 https://www.iamsterdam.com/en/our-network/amsterdam-and-partners/ news/2018/enjoy-and-respect
15 https://www.independent.co.uk/travel/news-and-advice/amsterdam-let ters-removed-tourism-netherlands-rijksmuseum-a8669901.html
16 https://www.theguardian.com/world/2018/jan/26/dutch-cheese-heads-told-to-close-amsterdam-shop

Bright Lights, Big City

1 https://denisdoeland.com/dance-festival-monitor-2017/
2 https://www.amsterdam-dance-event.nl/static/files/dance-onomics_ economic-significance-edm-17102012.pdf
3 https://www.anothermag.com/art-photography/7826/behind-the-scenes-at-andy-warhols-silver-factory

Biographies

Architectural historian **Esther Agricola** is the Director of Urban Planning and Sustainability at the City of Amsterdam. Previously, she headed the Amsterdam Bureau for Heritage and Archeology.

Journalist **Daan Dekker** is the author of *De Betonnen Droom (The Concrete Dream)*, (Thomas Rap, 2017) a biography of de Bijlmer and its designer, Siegfried Nassuth. He works as a programmer at Pakhuis de Zwijger, a centre for urban debate.

Legal scholar and philosopher **Menno van der Veen** is one of the founders of Tertium, an office for strategic communication and citizen participation, and a researcher at the University of Amsterdam. He is author of various novels, most recently *Ontweten*, (Van Oorschot, 2019).

Architect **Marc Schmit** is the co-founder of playze, an international architecture firm with offices in Berlin, Zurich and Shanghai.

Architect **Florian Idenburg** is the co-founder of Brooklyn-based architecture firm SO-IL. His research on the future of work will be published in the forthcoming book *Human(s) Work, the Office of Good Intentions*, (Taschen, 2019), co-authored with LeeAnn Suen.

Architects **Selva Gürdoğan and Greger Thomsen** are co-founders of Superpool, a research and architecture firm based in Istanbul. In the same city, they also headed Studio-X, an urban laboratory established by Columbia University Graduate School of Architecture, Planning and Preservation.

Valerie von der Tann is general manager at ViaVan Berlin. She is previously of McKinsey Berlin, where she co-led a global research study on liveable smart cities for think-tank, the McKinsey Global Institute.

Neville Mars is the founder of Shanghai-based firm, MARS Architects, as well as think-tank, Dynamic City Foundation. He is the author of *The Chinese Dream* (010 Publishers, 2008), and the forthcoming book, *The Manifesto of Mistakes*.

Architect **Inge Goudsmit** is Associate at OMA Hong Kong. In 2014 she started her project *'Boring Hong Kong,'* a research into the sociological consequences of the territory's mega housing estates.

Architect **Adam S. Frampton** is the founder of Only If, an architecture firm based in New York City. He is the co-author of *Cities without Ground* (ORO, 2012), a book on the urban landscape of Hong Kong.

Architect **Miguel Gentil Fernández** is the co-founder of Baum Arquitectura, a research and architecture firm based in Seville.

Tourism expert **Stephen Hodes** studied urban planning before specializing in the field of tourism. He is a partner at the Dutch LAGroup, a consultancy firm for culture and leisure.

David Mulder van der Vegt is an architect and the co-founder of Amsterdam-based architecture, urban planning, and research agency, XML. The office has published various books, including *Olympic Cities* and *Parliament*.

Acknowledgements

The Amsterdam Agenda began with an unstable Skype call from Syracuse airport, New York. Initiated by the Head of Urbanism of the Amsterdam Academy of Architecture, Markus Appenzeller, this was the start of the idea of an 'international lecture series.'

Back in Amsterdam, it was school Director, Madeleine Maaskant, who pushed the project through and encouraged us to execute the venture in full swing. The support and trust of Markus, Madeleine, and of Jan-Richard Kikkert - the Head of Architecture at the Academy - was critical for the start of this project.

Throughout the spring of 2018, we invited 13 speakers from all over the globe to the Academy of Architecture in Amsterdam. All of them were willing to travel to the Dutch capital to share their thoughts and work. From intimate dinners in Madeleine's office, to truly energizing evenings with mesmerizing lectures and lengthy conversations, often continued afterwards at a downtown bar, speakers' engagement with our project was both humbling, and inspiring. We thank every single one for their enormous amount of energy, insights, and ideas.

During the lecture series, we collaborated with debate centre, Pakhuis De Zwijger, to have some lectures reach an even wider audience, including the series' concluding conference. As always, director Egbert Fransen provided us with a warm welcome and boundless enthusiasm.

Turning this lecture series into a book was easier said than done. Publisher Marcel Witvoet saw the potential of the project immediately, and it was our pleasure to once again work with him and his team at nai010.

After a decade of research and collaboration on emerging megacities, it was great to finally focus on our hometown, Amsterdam. We now look forward to our next endeavour.

Michiel Hulshof & Daan Roggeveen

nai010 publishers is an internationally orientated publisher specialized in developing, producing and distributing books in the fields of architecture, urbanism, art and design. www.nai010.com

nai010 books are available internationally at selected bookstores and from the following distribution partners:

North, Central and South America -
Artbook | D.A.P., New York, USA, dap@dapinc.com

Rest of the world -
Idea Books, Amsterdam, the Netherlands, idea@ideabooks.nl

For general questions, please contact nai010 publishers directly at sales@nai010.com or visit our website www.nai010.com for further information.

Printed and bound in the Netherlands

ISBN 978-94-6208-542-8

Also available as e-book (pdf)
The Amsterdam Agenda (pdf)
ISBN 978-94-6208-543-5